L'Chaim, Sarah Jane!
During your life may you learn to love
and appreciate herbs
as much as I.

ANGUS & ROBERTSON PUBLISHERS

*Unit 4, Eden Park, 31 Waterloo Road,
North Ryde, NSW, Australia 2113 and
16 Golden Square, London W1R 4BN,
United Kingdom*

*First published in Australia
by Angus & Robertson Publishers in 1985
First published in the United Kingdom
by Angus & Robertson (UK) Ltd in 1985
Reprinted 1987*

*Copyright © Shirley Reid 1985
Copyright © Derek Cork, illustrations
on pp 6, 8, 10, 11, 12 16, 17, 18, 19,
22, 23 (right and left column), 27, 28,
30, 38, 39, 41, 46, 47*

*National Library of Australia
Cataloguing-in-publication data.*
Reid, Shirley
  Herbs for the home and garden.
  ISBN 0 207 15105 9.

  1. Herb gardening. 2. Cookery (Herbs).
  I. Title.
635'.7

Typeset in Tiffany by Setrite Typesetters, Hong Kong
Printed in Hong Kong

CONTENTS

ACKNOWLEDGEMENTS

My thanks go to my son-in-law, Rob Johnston, for his
care and dedication in taking the photographs for
this book.
I must also mention the kindness of Jan and Michael
Bailes, who gave gracious permission for Rob to
photograph their beautiful "Fragrant Garden" at
Erina, N.S.W.

HERBS – AN INTRODUCTION
1

"And God said: Let the earth bring forth grass, the herb yielding seed, and the fruit tree yielding fruit after his kind, whose seed is in itself upon the earth: and it was so." (*Genesis* 1: 11)

Herbs are mentioned often in the Bible and have been, since earliest times, an essential part of humanity's existence. Used for food, in the case of the large-leafed types such as borage, in medicines and beauty aids, as part of religious ceremonies, for sanitation, and as natural insect repellents, they became obvious trading commodities. The bartering of different herbs led to the spread of varieties throughout the world.

Many plants regarded today as vegetables were in earlier times known as "pot herbs" as they were used in cooked dishes. Among these, and recommended by Charlemagne the Great as essential to a healthy diet, were cucumber, beans, lettuce, celery, sugar beets, parsnips, carrots, kohlrabi, cabbage, onions, leeks, radishes, artichokes, broad beans and peas. In the twelfth century a great ten-part poem was written by the Abbot of the Augustines at Cirencester, and in Book 7 he praised the value of herbs such as plantain, wormwood, betony and centaury. He described his concept of a noble garden in another work titled *De Naturis Rerum*. It "should be adorned with roses, lilies, turnsole, violets and mandrake; there you should have parsley and fennel and southernwood and coriander, sage, savory, hyssop, mint, rue, dittany, smallage, pellitory, lettuce, garden cress, paeonies. There should be planted beds with onions, leeks, garlick, pumpkins, and shalots, cucumber, daffodils and acanthus should be in a good garden. There should also be pottage herbs such as beets, herb mercury, orach, sorrel and mallows."

The monks of early Christianity and through the centuries followed in the footsteps of famous Greek physicians and philosophers of old, notably Hippocrates, Theophrastus, and Dioscorides, who in about A.D. 77 wrote his *De Materia Medica*, which was the basis for medical treatment throughout Western Europe until the end of the sixteenth century. At this time translations were printed of the remarkable works of Galen, a brilliant Greek physician who lived from about A.D. 130 to 200 and who had refined the use of herbal cures. The monks grew herbs in their monastery gardens for the treatment of illnesses and ailments of all kinds and were virtually the only medical help in many areas.

An account of a Saxon monastery garden describes the "hortus", which was a rectangular enclosure with a central path leading from the gardener's house and shed where the tools were kept and, more interestingly, the "herbaularis", the small physic garden with a border of plants along the enclosing wall and four beds either side of the central pathway. Each plant was clearly and precisely labelled. Some of the Saxon names which had a Latin derivative were coriander, cumin, chervil, fennel, lovage, feverfew, mint, parsley, poppy, mustard and rue.

Many of the garden plants prized today for their beautiful flowers were used in earlier times for flavouring, medicine, beauty aids and in religious ceremonies. Examples are roses, violets, carnations, poppies, calendulas, lilies and lavender.

More than 2000 years ago an elegant and luxury-loving race known as Sybarites lived in Sybaris. The citizens of this opulent city slept on beds of fresh uncrushed rose petals and were so fond of rich sauces with their various foods that they rewarded very well indeed anyone who developed a new delicious sauce featuring herbs.

The violet was highly regarded in ancient Athens and was used in any number of ways to enhance foods, wines and living conditions. Wreaths of this dainty flower (as with roses) were worn at banquets to ward off drunkenness. Violets were strewn on floors of public buildings and temples and, being the emblem of Athens, were etched on pavements.

When the Athenian citizen attended a public bath an attendant would rub various appropriate herbs on different parts of the body. For example, mint, the symbol of strength, was used on the arms, thyme on the chest as a symbol of courage and every virtue. Indeed, to be said to "smell of thyme" was a popular accolade to signify high praise of virtue in Athens.

Sprays of pungent herbs were burnt on altars of temples. Herbs were used to add fragrance to bath water and were strewn in the streets to give an agreeable aroma to the air. Bees were pastured on fields of particualr herbs to flavour their honey. Even today thyme honey is very popular and well known in Greece.

Much superstitious belief involved various herbs. In classical mythology, various deities had herbs of different kinds dedicated to them. For example, bay was dedicated to Apollo.

The Romans were as devoted to the use of herbs as were the Greeks and used them in every possible way. For those who could afford the then high price of lavender this fragrance bringer was used to perfume both bath and bather. The word "lavender" in fact comes from the Latin *lavare* — to wash. Egypt was the main supplier of roses and shiploads were imported to satisfy the demands of the Roman citizenry. Vast nurseries were set up in Italy to grow them also and for out-of-season blooms these nurseries were equipped with networks of heating pipes warmed by hot water. The Romans particularly favoured rose petals for marriage beds. Roses were used in salads and as garnishes for food, while garlands were placed on pillars. Rose and violet wines were as popular with the Romans as with the Greeks. Carnations, as well as numerous other flowers, were used for decoration, cooking and wine brewing. That favourite liqueur, chartreuse, numbers among its ingredients balm, hyssop, carnation and angelica as well as many other herbs. Parfait Amour and L'Huile de Rose, two popular and delicious French liqueurs, are flavoured with roses.

Much was expected from Roman chefs and many applications of herbs which we use in today's cooking originated in Roman kitchens. It was the Romans who discovered the delicious delight of mint sauce and experimented with combinations of other herbs, vegetables and meats.

After the fall of Rome, during the period known as the Dark Ages, the finer points of good cooking languished, especially in the British Isles where invading Saxons almost completely wiped out the Roman – British culture, leaving beautiful villas in ruins and allowing herb gardens and orchards to revert to the wild. Eventually, however, the Middle Ages dawned, and travellers ventured forth from Britain to the Continent. Here they acquired a taste for French fare and wines as well as other refinements. Becoming great herb fanciers, they used over 500 different varieties in foods and medicines, while 100 fewer were deemed useful on the Continent.

Much trafficking in herbs took place as the years passed. Some of the monasteries began to sell the surplus produce from their herb gardens to the public to defray the cost of running the gardens. Until the fourteenth century the monasteries provided the only infirmaries for the sick and the only safe and desirable inns for the traveller in Britain. Englishmen touring the Continent returned with reports of inns established there which provided not only excellent food and wine, but pillows stuffed with violets or herbs, herb mouth rinses, and rose-water with which to bathe the face.

The Crusaders returned to medieval England with further refinement as well as new herbs, spices and flowers. Ladies embroidered scarves for the knights they favoured, or their lords, with sprays of thyme and borage, the symbols of courage.

During the early years of the Hundred Years War with France, plunder and captured French nobles were taken to England. While these reluctant "guests" waited for ransoms to be paid, they introduced further French "refinements" into the households of their captors.

The insect-repelling qualities as well as the delightful aroma of herbs had long been appreciated and clothes chests were fitted with special *garde de robe* compartments to both sweeten clothing and to deter moths and silverfish. The bed chambers were richly embellished with sprays of aromatic herb foliage, not only in bedding but also in the form of garlands and nosegays. These were also placed, fresh, in all inside living areas.

Henry III was so charmed and impressed by the efficiency of herbs that in 1251 he ordered the wall outside the royal bed chamber at Guildford Palace to be removed and rebuilt five metres away to provide space for a herb garden between the chamber and the wall.

London during the Middle Ages was very herb-conscious. Almost all churches, large buildings and homes were whitewashed to weatherproof them and often they were decorated, for both superstitious and religious reasons, with wreaths of herbs and flowers. The gateway to St Paul's Churchyard was the scene of a herb market where the gardeners employed by the nobility and wealthier citizens sold herbs. Herb women sang in the streets, crying their wares, having gathered wild herbs in the countryside. No doubt many a hawker trod Camomile Street in Bishopsgate.

The herb sellers of old London added their cry of "Rosemary and sweetbriar" to the voices of other vendors.

Posies and nosegays of aromatic herbs were carried to mitigate the stench of poor sanitation and the heaps of refuse dumped in the streets. Benches and tables were assiduously rubbed with odorous herbs, food on all occasions was flavoured with them and sprays were scattered on floors in banqueting chambers so that replete diners, most wearing chaplets of herbs, often slept on these fragrance-strewn areas. Centuries later the English herbalist, John Gerard, referring to mint, wrote: "The smell rejoiceth the heart of man, for which cause they used to strew it in chambers and places of recreation, pleasure and repose, where feasts and banquets are made."

Pilgrims venturing to English and continental shrines took with them insect-deterring herbs and those returning to England from the Continent brought with them a taste for more exotic foods and a knowledge of further uses of herbs in medicine and cooking.

Herbs such as rosemary, lavender and santolina were favoured as border plants in the knot gardens of Tudor England. Knots, such as the one pictured, were beds laid out in elaborate patterns, planted with low evergreen shrubs and herbs.

Tudor England saw an upsurge in the use of herbs. The herbery was indispensable to every housewife. Herbs were needed for home nursing, for the kitchen and for the "still room" where cosmetics, toilet waters, "sweete bags", syrups, ointments, salves, wines, cordials, conserves, sachets, perfumed candles and the like were prepared. In addition to being cooked with herbs, food was garnished with them for serving and usually accompanied by herb sauces. Game, poultry, fish, various meats, heron, swan, peacock, and even turkey newly introduced from Mexico, were stuffed with seasonings flavoured with herbs. Puddings, desserts,

jellies and sweetmeats all owed their delicious taste to herbs.

Navigators, honest sailors and buccaneers took back to England with them new and exotic plants. The Reverend William Harrison in the latter part of the sixteenth century was so moved by the sight of all this exotica that he wrote: "It is a world also to see how many strange herbs, plants and annual fruits are daily brought unto us from the Indies, Americas, Tapabrane [Sri Lanka as it is now known], Canary Isles, and all parts of the world." He claimed that he grew 300 unusual plants in his "three hundred foot of ground" and admired the virtues of "Hampton Court, Nonsuch and Tibault's Cobham Garden". Harrison also remarked on the continuing improvement of English cuisine and attributed it to the chefs employed by English nobility, describing them as being "musical headed French-men and strangers" who, as old records reveal, made full use of culinary herbs.

Special apothecaries' shops were set up, stocking all manner of herbs, fresh and dried, and a wide range of herbal products. Mint, for example, was well represented with supplies of both fresh and dried mint, mint water, conserve of leaves, syrup of mints, "chimical oyle" and simple oil.

The physic garden was an essential part of any household and we are told in an old poem:

Good Aqua Composita, vinegar tart,
Rose water and treacle to comfort the hart,
Cold herbs in hir garden for agues that
    burn,
That over strong heat to good temper may
    turn.

Get water of fumentorie,
Liver to coole
And others the like or else lie like a foole
Conserve of the Barkerie,
Quinces and such
With sirops that easeth the sickly so much.

As immigrants left Britain and the continental countries, they took with them seeds, cuttings and root divisions of herbs, carefully packed, in order to have in their new countries those commodities that formed an essential part of their daily lives.

It was in this manner that a great many of the herbs we use today were transported to America, Australia and other colonies. Greatly prized not only for their value in the kitchen, herbs also were important for their curative qualities in new colonies short of medical help. Many were also used as dyeing agents and, of course, for cosmetic purposes.

The Victorians used herbs almost as assiduously as did their forefathers. Culinary herbs were in fact used constantly until the dawning of the twentieth century. As the years passed the interest in and knowledge of herbs lessened, but it is interesting to note that the physic gardens of yore were the "parents" of the botanical gardens of today, and that many modern medical formulas retain the use of constituents of culinary herbs.

It is possible for almost everyone to experience the joy of growing herbs. Some are fortunate enough to have sufficient room to establish a formal herb garden, others are limited to spots here and there among existing plantings of shrubs, trees and so on, but even flat dwellers can grow numerous varieties in pots on balconies or in window boxes. Many herbs will grow satisfactorily even inside a sunny room.

Why not indulge yourself with these gifts of nature, and enjoy the magic of herbs in your home and garden.

HERB LORE
2

Angelica
Angelica archangelica

Angelica, which was known as "The Root of the Holy Ghost", was thought to prolong life if chewed. Perhaps this could be the elixir of life sought through the ages. The name angelica was given to this herb as the result of a vision in which the Archangel Gabriel recommended its use in the treatment and prevention of plague. In days gone by angelica was popular with herbalists as a stimulant, but this use seems to have lost favour in more modern times.

    Culpeper, the great astrology-conscious herbalist, wrote of this herb's medicinal value, and Parkinson, apothecary to James I, in his famous *Paradisi in Sole Paradisus Terrestris* written in 1629, claimed angelica to be one of the most effective medicinal herbs.

    From seed to root the whole plant has a delightful fragrance, reminiscent of muscatel grapes. The resinous gum obtained from the roots is often used in the manufacture of perfume as a substitute for musk benzoin. Angelica is used so frequently in the brewing and distillation of such a variety of wines and liqueurs, it could almost be called "The Herb of Bacchus"! It is suspected that the superb flavour of muscatel grapes in some Rhine wines is added by the secret and judicious use of angelica. It is also one of the herbs used in such liqueurs as absinthe, which also features wormwood. Seeds and ground root are used in kummel, the seeds are used to add flavour to gin and vermouth, while the dried leaves are incorporated in the mixing of bitters.

    The tender leaves are sometimes boiled and served as a celery-like vegetable. In Iceland, stems and roots are both eaten raw with butter, and the Laplanders peel the stalks and eat them with great relish. In Finland the healthful stimulating tea made from the infused leaves, either dried or fresh, is appreciated and the Finns also enjoy the young stems of angelica baked in hot ashes. The Norwegians use the roots to make a very special type of bread. A most remarkable and useful herb!

Balm
Melissa officinalis

Balm, with its lemony fragrance and flavour, was believed by Paracelsus, a Swiss physician of the sixteenth century, to restore "new life" to anyone taking it. His belief was endorsed in 1696 by an article in the *London Dispensary* which stated, "An essence of Balm, given in Canary wine, every morning will renew youth, strengthen the brains, relieve languishing nature and prevent baldness." An earlier edition affirmed that "Barme" was recommended as a cure for many afflictions including the bites of dogs, wry necks and "King's Evil".

    John Evelyn, a keen English herbalist wrote, "Balm is sovereign for the brain, strengthening the memory and powerfully chasing away melancholy." We are commanded by Culpeper: "Let a syrup be made with the juice of it and sugar be kept in every gentlewoman's house, to relieve the weak stomachs and sick bodies of their poor sickly neighbours." Dioscorides and fellow physicians of ancient times advised that wounds could be dressed with balm without "peril of inflammation". Pliny was even more effusive when he, extolling the herb's powers of healing, claimed: "It is of so great a virtue that though it be but tied to his sword that giveth the wound, it stauncheth the blood", though I cannot imagine too many soldiers tying it to their swords to staunch their adversaries' bleeding! Gerard, in agreement with Pliny's claim, asserted that "The juice of Balm glueth together greene wounds."

It seems that balm gives the gift of longevity to those who use it constantly. It is on record that, in Britain, a prince of Glamorgan, who lived to 108, always took herb teas containing a predominance of balm for breakfast. A gentleman of Sydenham, England, John Hussey, for fifty of his 116 years breakfasted on balm tea sweetened with honey. Balm, or melissa tea as it is also known, soothes nerves and relieves tension.

Balm was the apiastrum of the Romans, who regularly placed sprays in their hives to attract bees. Gerard stressed that "It is probably planted where bees are kept." Balm is also the main ingredient in the famous French Carmelite water that is made to this day.

Balm leaves finely chopped add zest to tossed salads and interesting flavour to soups, stews and poultry seasonings. In the Netherlands, balm foliage is used in the preparation of pickled eels and herrings. The leaves may also be dried and used in sachets, potpourris, sweet bags and herb pillows.

Basil
Ocimum sp.

No herb has aroused as much controversy as basil. Parkinson describes it as having "the smell so excellent that it is fit for a King's house". He also shared a superstition with many very early herbalists, writing: "It is also observed that scorpions doe rest and much abide under these pots and vessells wherein Basil is planted." Another curious superstition was that if basil was smelled closely it would be the cause of a scorpion rising in the brain! I have many times sniffed deeply at a pot of fresh basil and even broken sprigs to rub on my skin as a natural fly deterrent and I am still waiting for that scorpion. Culpeper was obviously confused by various ancient beliefs and reports that "Galen and Dioscorides told it is not fitting to be taken inwardly and Chrysippus rails at it. Pliny and the Arabians defend it. Something is the matter, this herb and rue will not grow together, no, nor near one another, and we know rue is as great an enemy to poison as any that grows."

Parkinson reported in the seventeenth century that "The ordinary Basil is in a manner wholly spent to make sweete or washing herbs among other sweet herbs, yet sometimes it is put into nosegays. The physicall properties are to procure a cheerfull and merry hearte whereunto the seeds are chiefly used in powder."

On the Continent, however, basil was favoured as well as for its aromatic qualities, as a distinctive culinary herb and for its medicinal uses. One interesting use was recorded by a Belgian herbalist, Dodoens, who wrote that many people believed that "A woman in labour, if she but hold in her hand a root of this herb together with the feather of a swallow, shall be delivered without pain."

In areas of Romania it was reputed through long tradition that any youth would, immediately and for all time, love a maiden from whose hand he had taken a spray of basil. It was considered a love token in Italy and in Crete was regarded as a symbol of "love washed with tears". Egyptians strewed basil flowers on the graves of their relatives while in Malaysia and Persia (now Iran), basil was planted by mourners on the graves of their loved ones.

The ancient Greeks, conversely, believed basil represented not only misfortune but also hatred. Their illustration of poverty took the form of a beggar-woman with sad face dressed in ragged clothing with a pot of basil at her side. They believed it to be useless to attempt to sow the herb unless with abuse and curses. The Romans agreed with them, and while using it as a strewing and scent herb, believed it would not flourish unless reviled during planting.

In Tudor times basil was valued for its "clovey" perfume and it was considered a compliment to be given a small pot of this herb. It was first grown in English gardens in the sixteenth century and soon became a favourite kitchen herb. It was used extensively to add fragrance to royal unguents, perfumes and medicines. All basils are useful in medicine to counteract fevers and kidney and bladder upsets. They add delicious flavour to Italian foods, tomato dishes, soups, sauces, sausages and rich stews. Widely available are sweet basil, growing to about 60–80 centimetres tall, bush basil, the baby of the family as it only reaches 30 centimetres in height, and Dark Opal Basil, which attains a height of 60 centimetres and has dark purple foliage which is both decorative and edible.

Bay
Laurus nobilis

This must be the most noble of herbs, if only because of its size. Bay trees will attain a height of 11 to 12 metres in a temperate climate. Always well sought after by connoisseurs, this herb is appreciated for its appearance as well as the flavour of its dark green leathery leaves, which may, like all herbs, be used fresh. So often I've been asked during lectures if the leaves must be dried prior to use and the answer is a firm "no!"

In Tudor times Parkinson wrote regarding bay: "It serveth to adorn the House of God, as well as of man; to procure warmth, comfort, and strength, to the limmes of men and women by bathings and anoyntings." Culpeper endorsed the use and virtues of bay when he described it as "resisting all evils which old Satan can do to man, and they are not a few . . ."

The English term Poet Laureate comes from the Roman habit (bay originated in Italy) of crowning victors in sports and poetic competitions with chaplets of bay leaves, and bay leaves are included in the badges of the Royal Air Force.

Christina McDonald, a New Zealand herbalist, records seeing a horse-drawn farm cart led by a man and loaded with branches of bay. The cart contained the body of an RAF officer being brought back to be buried in the village in which he had lived.

We are told by the Dutch physician and herbalist, De Gubernates that the Greeks believed the god of the sun wore the laurel, as the bay is also known, which reputedly was luminous and, like the god, had the power to bestow light, fame and glory. It was because of these light-giving

qualities that it was used in connection with the oracles. The Pythonesses ate the leaves to assist them to prophesy, while those who visited them seeking help were crowned with the leaves.

An Arabian herbalist, Ibn Baithar, gave a remarkable preventive for drunkenness. His advice was to pluck a single bay leaf and without allowing it to fall to the ground place it behind your ear. This, it was thought, will prevent a person being affected by wine. The theory presumably does not extend to martinis and bloody marys!

The bay is slow to develop and quite costly. Many people prefer to grow bay trees in pots, particularly in cold climates, and to keep them clipped or "poodled", so leaves may be easily obtained for bouquet garni and to flavour all manner of stews, poultry dishes, soups and, strangely, milk puddings and sauces. The flavour is very strong, so a little caution is advisable — in some cases half a leaf may be sufficient.

Bergamot
Monarda didyma

Around the middle of the eighteenth century an American "swamp plant" was introduced into England. Known as bergamot, Oswego tea plant, or bee balm, its botanical name *Monarda didyma* was given in honour of a famous Spanish botanist-priest, Nicholas Monardez. The common names, however, refer to the attributes of this herb. "Bergamot" refers to its aroma which is reminiscent of the bergamot orange. It was found in abundance in the dampish areas of Oswego, around Lake Ontario, and Indians and white settlers alike brewed a fragrant tea from the leaves. Bees swarm around the honeysuckle-like flowers of reddish-mauve which are redolent in nectar. Dr Nicholas Monardez mentioned this herb and other botanical discoveries in his book *Joyful News out of the New Founde World* which was translated into English in 1577. The first plants raised in England were

pensiveness and melancholy: it helpeth to clarify the blood and mitigate heat in fevers." Other herbalists believed it to be useful in the treatment of pulmonary and kidney complaints. The ancient Greeks and Romans made a practice of placing sprays of borage in wine cups, no doubt to "make men and women glad and merry", as Gerard tells us borage will. Certainly the foliage used in this way does actually cool drinks and has a delightful invigorating effect.

Originating as a wild plant in Aleppo, Syria, borage soon became naturalised all over Europe. The ancient Greeks believed it to be a symbol of courage — Dutch, no doubt, obtained from those wine cups! — and the blue starry flowers became a favourite embroidery design in the Middle Ages. Borage sometimes alternates the colour of its flowers and it is not uncommon to find a plant bearing blue, pink and white blooms simultaneously. There is an old English

from seed sown by Peter Collinson in 1745, after it was collected from the shores of Lake Ontario and sent to him by a well-wisher.

The leaves and flowers both dry well and, retaining their fragrance, are suitable to use in sachets, potpourri and sweet bags. The tea made from the leaves is refreshing and healthful. The flowers look lovely floated in punches and fruit drinks, and, torn, in tossed salads. Soak the flowers in cold water prior to using — their nectar content is so high tiny insects love to "raid the larder" of sweetness.

Borage
Borago officinalis

Borage was recommended by Culpeper when he wrote: "The leaves and roots are to very good purpose used in putrid and pestilential fevers to defend the heart, and to resist and expel the poison or venom of other creatures ...", and also when he advised that "The leaves, flowers and seed, all or any of them are good to expel saying that "a garden without borage is a garden without corage". A stirrup cup containing leaves of borage was offered to Crusaders as they set forth on their journeys. There is another old theory that the botanical name of this hairy herb was once "Corago" rather than "Borago". The Latin *cor* covers a kaleidoscope of meanings — heart, understanding, courage, soul and purpose.

Many local names have been given to this beautiful old plant: a herb of gladness, cool tankard; to the French it is *langue-de-boeuf*, while yet another name, bee bread, indicates its great appeal to bees. With its delicate cucumber flavour, the young leaves are popular in salads, and these young leaves, together with the shoots, are boiled as a pot herb. The flowers make an appealing garnish whether used fresh or crystallised. If candied, they may also be served as a sweetmeat with after-dinner coffee.

Burnet, Salad
Sanguisorba minor

Burnet, that *pimpinella*, is considered an invaluable salad herb in French and Italian kitchens. In Sweden it was often prescribed to aid those suffering from convulsive and spasmodic disorders. Gerard had much the same opinion of burnet, or salad burnet as it is more commonly known, as he did of borage and recommended it: "To make the hart merry and glad, as also being put into wine, to which it yieldth a certain grace in the drinking." Again like borage, the slender fine incised leaves of burnet taste of cucumber. They are excellent in sandwiches, salads of course, and accentuate the flavour of other herbs when combined with them in soups and stews.

Yet another English herbalist, Turner described salad burnet in his *Newe Herball* written in 1551: "It has two little leaves like unto the wings of birdes, standing out as the bird setteth her wings out when she intendeth to flye. Ye

Dutchmen call it flengottes berdlen, that is, God's little birde, because of the colour that it hath on topp." This remark referred to the crimson colour of the stigma.

Pliny recommended a decoction of burnet beaten together with honey for many physical problems. The ancients accorded it much faith and belief in its medical powers and it was thought to give protection against the infection of plague and other contagious illnesses. Judged to be a great healing herb, it was taken internally as well as being used in ointments, and was credited with the relief of the rheumatism and gout of the Tudors.

Calendula
Calendula officinalis

The calendula or English marigold which so brightens gardens at the end of winter and heralds spring with such a symphony of golds and orange, has its place in the herb garden. It is a flower that has attracted many legends and is known in many countries. The Buddhists in India

consider it to be sacred to the Goddess Mahadeve. The trident emblem of this deity is decorated with marigold blooms and during festivals her devotees crown themselves with wreaths of the flowers. The Greeks also used it for decorations and it is believed that to dream of this beautiful sun-hued flower is to foretell marriage, success and riches. The reign of Henry VII saw baskets of orange, gold and lemon blooms sent by swains to the ladies of their choice. Mexicans, on the other hand, believe this bright flower to be a symbol of death and use it on sombre occasions to decorate churches. In old Germanic accounts the flower was called *Toutenblume*, meaning flowers of the dead, and was shunned.

The petals have been used as an adulterant or substitute for the more expensive saffron, and in fresh fruit or tossed salads. During the American Civil War a tincture of petals was used by surgeons and it was generally believed that a flower applied to a bee or wasp sting would relieve the pain.

Camomile (Chamomile)
Anthemis nobilis

Camomile was, we learn from an old Saxon manuscript was acclaimed: "Thys herbe was consecrated by the wyse men of Egypt unto the Sonne and was rekened to be the only remedy for all agues." Turner in the sixteenth century reported: "It will restore a man to hys color shortly if a man after the longe use of the bathe drynke of it after he is come forthe out of the bathe."

Culpeper believed that "The flowers boiled in posset-drink provoke sweat and help to expel all colds, aches and pains whatsoever." He also claimed that the ancient Egyptians used the herb with good effect.

It was found in early times and still is today growing wild over most of Europe and the mild regions of Asia. Growing quite flat, this pungent herb makes a fine lawn which will bear considerable traffic.

Indeed, the more it is trodden upon the better it grows, hence its title of "herb of humility". Turner wrote that "This herbe is scarce in Germany but in England it is so plenteous that it groweth not only in gardynes but also VII mile above London, it groweth in the wylde felds, in Richmonde grene, in Brantfurd grene." It is believed that camomile was introduced into Germany from Spain at the end of the Middle Ages.

The fragrance of this herb is very much like that of apples and the name is from the Greek *khamui*, meaning "on the ground"; the Spaniards refer to it as *manzanella*, meaning "little apple". Camomile is used in making some vermouths and light wines. It is a plant of a tremendous number of virtues. For centuries, and even today, camomile tea has been considered one of the most effective herbal teas useful for reducing fever, clearing skin eruptions and, applied cold, as an eyewash. The herb will also relieve toothache and neuralgia and the flowers are added to therapeutic herbal baths.

It was suggested by Francis Bacon in his famous *Essay on Gardens* that camomile was an excellent covering for garden paths. Because this former strewing herb is insect repelling, it is a

A happy combination of foliage and flower colour.
In the background the blue-mauve of borage in flower.
In the foreground grey-leafed santolina.

Top: Chervil, an important ingredient in the French *fines herbes*.
Bottom: Calendula petals make an attractive addition
to a tossed salad.

useful way of helping to keep flying insects away from leisure and pleasure areas.

Caraway
Carum carvi

Caraway was believed by Pliny to have originated in Caria, Asia, hence its name. Dioscorides recommended that pale-faced girls should improve their complexions by taking this herb. A very valuable medicinal herb, we are told by Culpeper, "The seed is conducing to all cold griefs of the head and stomach", and that it "helpeth to sharpen the eyesight". He also advises that the seed should be powdered and mixed into a poultice to take away the discolouration of bruises.

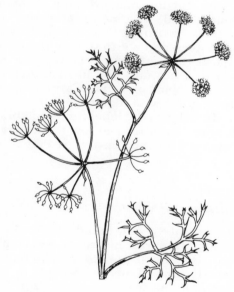

For centuries caraway has been appreciated and was one of the most popular herbs in classical times. All parts, root, fruit (seeds) and leaves, were used. The parsnip-like roots were mixed with milk and made into bread or eaten as a vegetable, while the leaves were used in salad and soups. Caraway seeds, rich in medicinal oil, were added to wines, cakes, breads and sweets. The ancient Arabs referred to the seeds as *karawga* and used them extensively. A traditional part of the English farm labourers' feast held at the end of the wheat sowing was caraway cake. In Norway and Sweden, the herb is also used to flavour bread, while in Germany, soups, cabbage and cheeses are all flavoured with the tangy seeds. The well-known liqueur, kummel, has caraway as its main flavouring essence and it is also used in several other cordials.

Superstition tells us that caraway has "holding power" and that if lovers drank a potion made from it they would not stray in their affections. Articles containing any part of the herb were believed to be safe from thieves. It has been proven in England that poultry and pigeons like the seeds and will stay close to home if they are provided with a lump of dough baked with caraway seeds mixed through.

Carnation
Dianthus caryophyllus

Theophrastus in the third century B.C. gave the name "dianthus", meaning "divine flower" to the lovely bloom we know as carnation. Originally a little "clove-pink", the present day carnation has been lovingly bred and developed. One of the oldest of garden flowers it was claimed by Pliny to have been found in Spain in the days of Augustus Caesar. Pliny referred to it as the *cantabrica* and also mentioned the Spanish use of spicing beverages with it.

The Romans and Greeks grew the carnation and the name itself comes from the Latin *carnatio*, which, as it means "flesh", probably alluded to the colour of the early "pinks". Members of both civilisations used this lovely flower to make garlands and floral wreaths for the head. In fact, the popular name of carnation was corrupted to "Coronation" due to the ancient custom of twining the flowers into betrothal crowns or chaplets worn by lovers as symbolic of the engagement of hearts, minds and hands.

The name carnation was first used by Henry Lyte in his translation of the brilliant *Histoire des Plants* compiled in 1557 by Rembert Dodoens of Antwerp. Other names were also applied to this clove-fragranced flower. It was known — particularly in Tudor times — as "gillyvors", "gillyflower" or "gilloflower", all of which were corruptions of the carnation's specific Latin name, *carophyllus*, which refers to the perfume of the flowers.

There are two theories about the introduction of this flower to England. One is that as it naturalises itself in rock fissures plants could have been taken over, unwittingly, in stone imported to England for the construction of Norman castles. In 1874 it was reported that "wild carnations" grew abundantly over a castle built by William the Conqueror. An earlier theory is that the Romans took plants with them among their collection of herbs when they invaded Britain. In any event, carnations quickly gained popularity.

As well as being used to spice ale, the carnation was used fresh or dried as a clothes' "sweetener" in clothes-presses and coffers. It was also used in nosegays either by itself or combined with other flowers to ward off unpleasant odours. In old paintings it may often be seen clasped lovingly in fingers to "be smelled so". Ladies used it as a motif for their embroidery and tapestry in Tudor times. They worked riotous sprays over garments, wall hangings, on the backs of fans, tablemats, book covers and cushions. The Stuarts also loved this flower and used it with abandon in their decorations.

The petals were dried for sachets, potpourri and herb pillows. They were also used to decorate salads and various other dishes and the clovey taste of the flower was appreciated in mulled wine or ale (the blooms were then known as "soppes-in-wine"). Often the petals were also candied for sweetmeats.

It was in Tudor times that the deep red carnation was favoured but Gerard wrote of yellow varieties that were introduced by Master Lete around 1580. Perdita in *The Winter's Tale* speaks of "streaked gilivers" as though they were well known in Tudor times.

In 1629 in his *Paradisi in Sole Paradisus Terrestris*, Parkinson listed nineteen varieties of carnations and thirty of pinks. Queen Henrietta Maria, wife of Charles I, gave them preference above other flowers and so increased their popularity. William Coles, a physician, in 1657 asserted that carnation cordial was efficacious "in fevers, expelling the poyson and fury of the disease, and greatly comforting those that are sick of any disease where the heart hath need of relief . . ." He describes a clove-pink vinegar to be used "to relieve one of a swoon", as later smelling salts were in the nineteenth century.

An Englishman, William Cobbett, obviously had a great preference for carnations, writing: "For my part, as a thing to keep and not to sell, as the thing, the *possession* of which is to give me pleasure, I hesitate not for a minute to prefer the plant of a fine Carnation to a gold watch set with diamonds."

In Bologna the inhabitants celebrate 29 June as Carnation Day and the flower is associated with the Feast of St Peter.

Chervil
Anthriscus cerefolium

This delicately flavoured herb is a particular favourite in France where it is known as *cerfeuil* and is considered an extremely important ingredient in the French *Fines herbes*.

Turner said of chervil: "If that it be eaten in a sallat or in a moose it is good for the stomache and head, by reason of the pleasant smell that it hath." As usual, Culpeper had his say and wrote that it could be used "to dissolve congealed or clotted blood in the body, or that which is clotted by bruises, falls, etc.; the juice or distilled water thereof being drunk and the bruised leaves laid to the place . . ."

Pliny also favoured the use of chervil as a medicinal plant and recommended that a decoction of the seed steeped in vinegar would cure hiccups.

Chervil is one of the oldest known flavouring plants and originated in Asia Minor and south-eastern Europe. The popularity of this herb is today quite extensive. As well as finding favour in French and American kitchens, it is also used in Germany and Austria as a seasoning for sausages and cold meats. As it enhances the flavour of other ingredients chervil is frequently included in cold jellied dishes, sauces and soups.

Chervil is a dainty herb and the delicate flower resembles Queen Anne's lace, making an effective garnish when floated on soup prior to serving.

Chives
Allium sp.

As with chervil, chives are among the finest herbs, and are always referred to in the plural. There are two varieties available — onion (*A. Schoenoprasum*) and garlic (*A. neapolitanum*) — and both add delightful flavour to all savoury dishes, salads and soups. Both the "grassy" leaves and tiny bulbs are edible, but it is usually only the tops that are harvested. The onion-like bulblets are often considered too small for general use and it is, of course, from them that further green spears of flavour shoot forth. It is a good idea to have a row of chives plants so that there are always plants to cut while others are recovering. Next to parsley, chives are probably the most universally used herb.

This herb has escaped from the kitchen garden and naturalised itself in rocky pockets on windswept cliffs in western Portugal, Corsica and Greece. It is used throughout the world. What jacket-baked potato would be complete without its sprinkling of chives on sour cream or butter? A popular flavour additive in Asia, chives have been used for centuries in China and Japan. Chives are also known as

rush leeks, the slender foliage being reminiscent of fine rushes, and in some countries are even referred to as chive "grass". Culpeper for once does not wax enthusiastic about a herb and in fact is quite derogatory. He claims "they send up very hurtful vapours to the brain, causing troublesome sleep". Considering how long in humanity's history this herb has been enthusiastically used, perhaps Culpeper was wrong! The Chinese believed it to be a valuable antidote to poisons and a remedy against bleeding.

Coriander
Coriandrum sativum

According to a Chinese belief, the seeds of coriander had the power to bestow immortality, and this herb is frequently referred to as "Chinese parsley". Peruvians used

both seeds and leaves to flavour food while ancient Egyptians used the leaves as a flavouring for soups. The Romans introduced coriander to Britain as they favoured it for its aromatic qualities. In some areas of the British Isles it has semi-naturalised itself. It was for a time grown commercially in Essex for the gin distillers and was also used as a drug by veterinarians in their treatment of animals. It is, of course, one of the bitter herbs taken at the Feast of Passover. The Italian herbalist, Varro, is quoted by Pliny as the authority who recommended sprinkling coriander lightly powdered with cumin, mixed with vinegar, over various meats to avoid summer spoilage.

When the dried seed is crushed it has a delightful fragrance and flavour. Medicinally the powdered seed is used to render drugs more palatable and small quantities of distilled coriander oil are sometimes added to eau-de-cologne. The oil is also used in liqueurs and cordials.

Coriander was described in the oldest English treatise on gardening, *The Feate of Gardening*, which was written in about 1440 by a Mayster Jon Gardener. Gerard described the herb thus: "The common kind of Coriander is a very striking herb, it has a round stalk full of branches, two feet long. The leaves are almost like the leaves of the Parsley, but later on become more jagged, almost like the leaves of Fumitorie, but a deal smaller and tenderer. The flowers are white and grow in round tassels like Dill."

It is coriander seed that is so important in Indian curry powder and the leaves are also used in many Indian dishes. Pliny long ago affirmed that the best coriander seeds were grown in ancient Egypt and imported to Rome.

Dandelion
Taraxacum officinale

In his *The Useful Plants of Great Britain* written in 1862, C. Pierpoint Johnson has some interesting things to tell us about the little-appreciated dandelion. For example, he writes of a famine caused by locust devastation in Menorca and how the people lived mainly upon the roots and leaves of the dandelion for many weeks. He informs us that a type of beer is fermented in Canada from this herb. It is also believed to be beneficial to cattle and will increase the milk of cows if included in their diet.

Originally, centuries ago, dandelion was grown for its flower and it is because of its compulsive self-seeding that it has become relegated to the "weed" status it holds in so many eyes. Medicinally, however, it has much value and is rich in iron and potassium. During the eighteenth century, the German physician and herbalist Dr Zimmerman used it as a cure for dropsy, his patient being no less a personage than Frederick, King of Prussia.

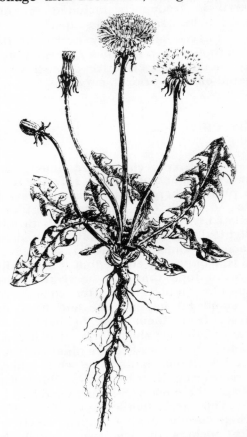

The Bible contains many references to this herb, which was known and appreciated by Arabian physicians. Serving humanity for centuries as a nutrient and medicine it remains in Europe a favourite salad herb — particularly in France. The plant may be blanched by placing over it an inverted terracotta plant pot with the drainage hole blocked. This makes the leaves more palatable for raw eating and the foliage is also excellent when steamed and served as a vegetable.

The head cook of James II stipulated at least thirty-two ingredients in a "simple" salad and a great many more in a "brave sallet". Almost always dandelion leaves were included. The plant has a very high nutritional value and contains calcium, sodium, silic acid, sulphur, potassium and vitamins A, B, C and D in its leaves. The root, which may be roasted and ground for a "herbal" coffee substitute, is rich in insulin. A well-known peasant wine is made from summer flowers and leaves and is recommended for relieving catarrh and rheumatism.

The name dandelion has led to much conjecture. There is, however, a reference to its appearance in the *Ortum Sanitatis* of 1485 which states "The herb was much employed by Master Wilhemus, a surgeon who, on account of its virtues, likened it to a lion's tooth ..." It does seem more logical to assume, however, that "dandelion" is a corruption of *dent-de-lion* — lion's tooth — which refers to the shape of the leaves. There are many common names applied in local areas to this sunny flower. Ben Jonson refers to it as "blowball", alluding to the children's game of telling the time by blowing the silvery puff away. An old rhyme tells us:

Dandelion with cloke of down
The schoolboy's clock in every town
Which truant puffs amain
To conjur lost hours back again.

Some of the English vernacular names are "peasant's clock", "canker wort", "Irish-daisy", "fortune teller", "one o'clock" and "doon-head clock".

Patrick Kavenagh in 1905 brought attention to the early germination habit of the dandelion when he wrote:

And over that potato field
A lazy veil of woven sun
Dandelions growing on headlands
Showing their unloved hearts to everyone.

Dill
Anethum graveolens

In the seventeenth century Michael Drayton wrote in *Nymphidia*, "There with her Vervain and her Dill, That hindereth witches of their will", referring to the supposed magical properties of this widely favoured herb. Dioscorides knew dill as "anethon" which he valued as a treatment for hiccups and flatulence, and in an Egyptian papyrus approximately 5000 years old it is reported as being used medicinally. A translation of Dodoen's herbal of 1578 said that dill was universally grown "amongst pot herbs and worts".

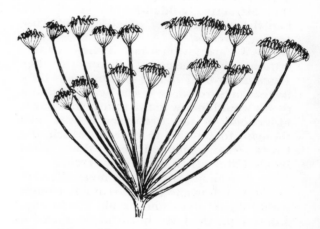

It was for centuries considered that wearing a spray of dill would bring good luck and in some countries many brides would place a spray of dill together with salt in their shoes and would often carry a posy of dill to their wedding.

Culpeper said this herb was under the dominion of Mercury and as a result, strengthened the brain. He wrote also, "The Dill being boiled and drunk is good to ease swellings and pains, it also stayeth the belly and stomach from casting", and advised a decoction of dill oil "to procure rest".

Joseph Addison in The *Spectator* wrote: "I am always pleased with that particular time of the year which is proper for the pickling of dill and cucumbers."

And indeed, recipes abound for using dill in such pickles as cucumbers, gherkins and cauliflowers. Joseph Cooper, chef to Charles I, left in his *Receipt Book* a recipe "To pickle Cucumbers in Dill". Later John Evelyn in his *Acetaria* of 1680, which was actually a book on "Sallets", gave his method for concocting "Dill and Colly-flower Pickle".

Elder
Sambucus nigra

There are probably more superstitions attached to the elder than to any other herb. Few old gardens were without one as this attractive golden-leafed small tree had the reputation of repelling and frus-trating witches.

We are given some of these super-stitions by Margaret Baker in her *Discovering the Folklore of Plants*. She tells us that in Shropshire it was believed that a death would follow in the family that burnt elderwood in the fireplace. It was also thought to be the tree from which the Cross was fashioned, and that Judas hanged himself from an elder tree.

It was never used for meat skewers or shipbuilding and furniture made from it would warp, crack and break. It was con-sidered particularly harmful to make a cradle from it as the tree spirit might attack the child. On the Scottish border it was believed that the elder would only flourish where blood had been spilt!

Elder branches were sometimes planted at gravesides to protect the dead. The leaves certainly keep the flies away and may be placed adjacent to open doors and windows for this purpose. Leaves gathered on the Eve of May Day were considered effective treatment for tooth-ache, melancholy and the bites of mad dogs and adders. Christopher Gullet wrote in 1772 that cabbages, turnips and fruit trees could be cleared of blight by being whipped with a bunch of elder twigs.

It has even been used as a cure for warts! A case is on record at Waddesdon,

Buckinghamshire, that earlier this century a girl was seriously affected by warts on her hands. A neighbour, secretly counting them, made a corresponding number of notches on an elder stick and buried it in the garden. This was done without the knowledge of the patient. As the stick rotted away, the warts disappeared, never to return. Elder was said to be an infallible protection against lightning and was often planted by stable doors to protect the cattle. A person was safe from all evil if elder was venerated and either planted nearby his or her dwelling or carried on the person. All in all, quite a remarkable herb!

All parts, wood, leaves, flowers and berries, were used for both food and medi-cine. The leaves and berries were used in syrups and decoctions and the flowers to make fritters and to flavour cordials. The berries were also used in brewing the famous elderberry wine.

Hippocrates prescribed the various parts for numerous illnesses and the Romans made a black hair dye from the berries. Elder was referred to by Culpeper: "It is needless to write any description of this, since every boy that plays with a pop-gun will not mistake another tree for the Elder." According to Audrey Hatfield in her *Pleasures of Herbs* a favourite old pickle was made of young elder shoots taken in spring and rendered into a *"Pickle in imitation of Indian Bamboo"*. The leaves may be pounded into a paste which is a useful healing agent. To repel flying insects dab elder-leaf tea on exposed skin. As the elderflower or leaf water has been renowned for centuries as a remarkable beauty aid, the skin must surely benefit.

Elderberry syrup taken with hot water will relieve the unpleasant sympt-oms of colds. The berries, in fact, possess very valuable medicinal qualities and various decoctions and concoctions made from them must be beneficial. At times they have been used to alleviate rheumatic and nerve pains, gout and dropsy. To gain full benefit from such a unique herb it is necessary to plant more than one, but a grove of this lovely plant will add interest and eye-appeal to any garden.

Fennel
Foeniculum vulgare

Believed to have slimming powers, the Greeks also attributed to fennel the ability to promote courage, strength and long life. The Romans made much use of it and ate the root, stem, leaf and seeds. They served it as a cooked vegetable or raw salad and used its seeds to flavour soups, breads, cakes, fish and other dishes. Pliny listed twenty-two ailments for which fennel was recommended as an effective treatment. He also recorded that to sharpen their sight, serpents rubbed their heads against the plant.

Charlemagne, that great emperor, ordered the cultivation of fennel on all imperial farms. Only good could come from it was the general belief, but again an old English superstition, "sow fennel, sow trouble", warns us that we should find fennel rather than cultivate it. To protect the sleepers, bedrooms or chambers had

the keyholes stuffed with fennel in the belief that this would prevent evil spirits from entering and disturbing those within. It was also entwined into the garlands which were hung over doors on that most potent season of witches, Midsummer Eve. The Romans and Greeks often twisted the herb among other foliage in victory wreaths.

During the eleventh century the household accounts of Edward I listed eight and a half pounds of fennel as being one month's supply, which will indicate how much appreciated was this herb. It was used generally during winter months to flavour fish that had been salted down for storage.

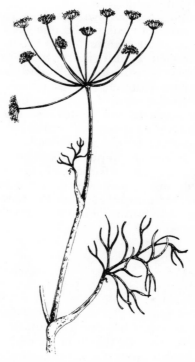

Parkinson in 1640 claimed that its culinary benefit was first realised in Italy, writing: "The leaves, seeds and rootes are both for meate and medicine; the Italians especially doe much delight in the use thereof and therefore transplant and whiten it, to make it more tender to please the taste, which being sweet and some- what hot helpeth to digest the crude qualitie of fish and other various meates. We use it to lay upon fish or to boyle it therewith and with divers other things, as also the seed in bread and other things."

I remember well an Italian who worked in our nursery. When delivering plants to a certain area he knew very well where there was a vigorous planting of wild fennel and would return gleefully with armloads of this aniseed-flavoured plant.

In 1650 William Cole wrote: "Both the seeds, leaves and root of our Garden Fennel are much used in drinks and broths for those that are grown fat, to abate their unwieldiness and cause them to grow more gaunt and lank."

Culpeper enjoyed the herb with fish: "One good old custom is not yet left off, viz., to boil fennel with fish for it consumes the phlegmatic humour which fish most plentifully afford and annoy the body with, though few that use it know wherefore they do it." A very old English recipe says to boil tender young fennel stems like "sparragrass" and to serve them with melted butter and vinegar.

Since it repels fleas and other annoying pests, fronds of fennel were placed among rushes and within bedding. Fennel tea may be used in the final rinsing water when bathing Fido to help relieve *his* flea problem.

Garlic
Allium sativum

This is one of the oldest and most widely used herbs in history. In fact, it has been used for so long that it is virtually imposs- ible to pinpoint its origin, though some evidence points to south-west Siberia. It was, however, firmly established through- out southern Europe from the beginning of recorded history.

It was even then appreciated for its value in flavouring food and in medicine and was also revered as a magical herb.

Old English beliefs tell us that the plant will draw moles from the earth and inspire roosters to fight. It was also believed that if a child was afflicted by measles, garlic was the cure. A piece of homespun linen was torn into nine pieces. Each piece was then spread with powdered garlic from nine cloves, and then wrapped around the child who was nursed for nine days. At dawn on the tenth day the linen was buried in the garden, whereupon the patient waited for the cure to follow!

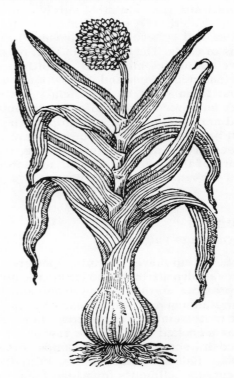

According to Pliny, when oaths were uttered in ancient Egypt, both garlic and onion were addressed as deities. In fact, in lower Egypt both were worshipped and regarded by many as being too holy to be eaten.

This did not prevent the builders of Cheops' great pyramid from being issued with vast quantities of garlic to eat. It also formed a main part of the Israelites' diet in Egypt. Greek and Roman soldiers and sailors were supplied with plentiful quantities as a health precaution while all rural classes in North Africa and Europe considered it one of their main foods.

The Roman, Horace, abhorred garlic, thinking it "more poisonous than Hemlock". Homer, the Greek poet, however, featured it as part of the menu at the feast served by the great hero of the Trojan War, Nestor, to his guest Machaon.

In ancient Greece, history tells us that anyone who had been eating garlic (and who is able to hide the fact?) was forbidden entrance to the temples of Cybele.

In some country areas peasants believed garlic possessed cooling powers against the heat of burning winds and sun when applied to the skin, a theory further supported in a travel book of more than a century ago: "The people in places where the Simoon is frequent eat Garlic and rub their lips and noses with it when they go out in the heat of summer to prevent their suffering from the Simoon."

The healing and medicinal qualities of garlic were discovered very early in its history. Galen described it as the rustic's "Theriac" or "Heal All", while Pliny gave a very long descriptive list of its curative attributes. It was praised by many including Dioscorides for cleaning the vocal cords. Culpeper as usual had *his* say regarding the value of garlic and after telling us, "Mars owns this herb", he went on with a very impressive list of complaints which could be relieved by either taking or applying garlic.

There is, of course, one characteristic of garlic which is far less to be admired and that is the smell! William Bullein in his *Book of Simples* remarked in 1562 that it was extremely unpleasant a medicine for "Fayre Ladyes", whom he considered to "preferre sweete breathes before gentle words".

Garlic is an effective disinfectant and vast quantities of it were used during the First World War to treat the wounded. A decoction known as "Four Thieves" Vinegar used to ward off the effects of plague during 1722 in Marseilles had

garlic as its main ingredient. It seems four convicted thieves asserted they had anointed themselves with the potion before robbing corpses of epidemic victims. During an outbreak of plague through the London slums in the nineteenth century, garlic-eating French priests were able to aid victims with impunity, while English clergy themselves became victims of the infection.

It seems strange that, with so much in favour of garlic, an old English country name was "Devil's Poxy", for it was believed that it had connections with the Evil One. In past centuries the Chinese used it as a protection against the Evil Eye. It was also used in Europe against vampires and evil spirits. Another interesting legend is that if a clove of garlic is planted beside a rose bush, the rose in sheer self-defence will develop a stronger perfume in its bloom!

There is an old country superstition that if a child wears a clove of garlic in a small cloth bag around the neck as an amulet, that child will be protected from whooping cough. My mother-in-law followed this practice with her daughter, but we wonder if sufferers from the complaint kept away from Betty because of her garlicky aroma and thus kept the infection to themselves!

Geranium
Pelargonium spp.

There are about 300 species of this vast family scattered over those areas in the world which are temperate. In our nursery we grow only those with definite fragrances — for example, apple, cinnamon, coconut, lemon (both variegated and plain green), lime, nutmeg, orange, peppermint and rose. All are edible and all add superb flavour to milk dishes, fondants and plain cakes. Some of those 300 species are grown in gardens, others grow only in their indigenous state and others have naturalised themselves in Britain, North America and Europe.

C. Pierpoint Johnson in *The Useful Plants of Great Britain* (1862) writes that all native geraniums are more or less astringent and that in Wales geranium is sometimes given in disorders of the kidneys. Sometimes referred to as herb Robert, the primitive form of our better known varieties of today was the "geranium" of the Middle Ages. Mayster Jon Gardener described it in his *The Feate of Gardening* and herb Robert was one of the delightful range of plants used for bordering gardens before being superseded by the less attractive box.

The oak-leafed geraniums originated in South Africa and were introduced into England in the seventeenth century. They quickly established a place for themselves as they are extremely accommodating. Whenever emigrants left British shores they took with them cuttings of this adaptable plant, spreading it throughout the Mediterranean area, America and Australia. Think of window boxes crammed with bright red geraniums along the Côte d'Azure!

It became a strong favourite in Victorian times — it was regarded as a status symbol — and was tended and clipped with meticulous care. Somehow it fitted in very well with the plush upholstery and bright red soldiers' uniforms of that era.

The leaves may be dried for including in sachets, potpourris, and so on, but seem to have little, if any, medicinal value.

There is a persisting legend regarding this versatile plant. It seems one day the prophet Muhammad after washing his shirt hung it on a mallow plant to dry. After removing the shirt he found that lovely plant had changed into a geranium. The geranium is sometimes given the nickname of "cranebill" or "storkbill", as the fruit bears a seed that resembles a bird's bill.

Horehound
Marrubium vulgare

This is a British native plant and is found throughout Wales, Ireland, Scotland and the eastern and southern coasts of England. It has also been discovered over central and western Asia, Europe and the Canary Isles. During Georgian times it was favoured when dried as a snuff.

It is one of the five bitter herbs of the Mishna of which the Jewish people partook during the Passover. Gerard suggested making a syrup from the fresh leaves as they are "a most singular remedie against the cough and the wheezing of the lungs ... and doth wonderfully well ease such as have been long sick of any consumption of the lungs, as hath been often proven by the learned physicians of our London College".

The leaves of this herb are the part used in an infusion drunk as a relief against bronchitis, coughs and colds and also for the treatment of jaundice and dyspepsia.

Culpeper wrote that the herb belongs to Mercury and suggests other ways of using it, for example, "The green leaves bruised and boiled in hog's grease into an ointment, heals the bites of dogs, abates the swollen part which comes by pricking thorns . . . The leaves used with honey purge foul ulcers, stay running and creeping sores."

Gypsies in Britain believe applications of horehound tea help to "keep flies from everlastingly tormenting on ye". Rather a change from aerosol fly deterrents and infinitely better for the skin and the environment.

Horseradish
Cochlearia armoracia

In his comprehensive herbal, Culpeper makes no reference to this herb. Evidently it was unknown to him. It was introduced from Italy to England and later to America and divisions of the root were taken to other countries by early settlers. Unlike most herbs, horseradish can only be propagated from root divisions.

Gerard knew the herb and wrote: "Horseradish for the most part groweth and is planted in gardens, yet have I found it wilde in sundrie places . . . Horseradish stamped, with a little vinegar put thereto, is commonly used among the Germans for sauce to eat fish with, and such like meates, as we do mustard." It took around 100 years for this herb to be accepted as a condiment in Britain, however. We know of course that roast beef and horseradish sauce is almost a British national dish today. In 1687 Robert Turner wrote in his *British Physician* that the herb is "under the dominion of Mars and is hot and dry in the third degree". He went on to say that it was eaten with fish and "other meats" like mustard.

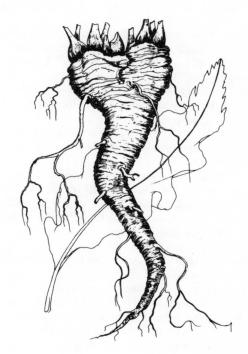

The leaves and more particularly the root contain the essential oil which gives the herb its pungency. Various physicians favoured its use. "Of all things given to children for worms, horseradish is not the least for it soon killeth and expelleth them," wrote one. Another prescribed it to treat scurvy when the fever was not high, while a third suggested "one drachm of horseradish, scraped, and made into a syrup with its own weight of sugar and four ounces of water" as a cure for hoarseness.

Hyssop
Hyssopus officinalis

Over 2000 years ago reference was made to this ancient herb in the 51st Psalm where it is written: "Purge me with Hyssop and I shall be clean." It was used for bringing fresh fragrance to temples and churches and also as a strewing herb in halls and palaces. Culpeper claimed this herb for Jupiter and wrote: "Hyssop boiled with honey and rue, and drank, helps those that are troubled with coughs and short-ness of breath, wheezing and rheumatic distillations upon the lungs . . ." Further on he claims: "The green herb bruised with sugar quickly heals any cut or green wounds, if properly applied. The pain and discolourings of bruises, blows and falls may be quickly removed by a cataplasm of the green leaves sewed in a linen cloth and put on the place."

John Ray, earlier than Culpeper, claimed much the same thing for hyssop in his *First British Flora* of 1670. In it he tells of a man who was savagely kicked on the thigh by a horse and immediately had a poultice of boiled hyssop applied. The pain ceased immediately and within a bare few hours all signs of bruising had disap-peared. A remarkable claim indeed, but one worth noting if a household has toddlers prone to tripping and stumbling and thus collecting the odd bruise or two.

Hyssop is a decorative herb to grow, with a low, upright habit, carrying deep green narrow leaves embellished by blue, white or pink flowers. It is often used as a border plant and trims well. Eleanor Sinclair Rohde tells us in her delightful *A Garden of Herbs* that old mazes were often "sette with isope", and that Tusser included hyssop in his lists of those herbs

to be used for strewing. If this plant is not kept trimmed it will tend to semi-prostrate itself but even then is still attractive.

The leaves, so Pliny reports, were formerly used in a wine known as hyssopites. The flowers may be used to brew a tea which will help relieve catarrh. The leaves, stems and flowers, when dis-tilled, will yield a fine oil prized even above oil of lavender by perfumers. Gerard supported Culpeper's claim for this pungent herb when he tells us that a "decoction of Hyssop is made with figges, water, honey and rue and drunken helpeth the old cough".

I like to use one or two leaves to flavour soups and stews. A tiny sprinkling on salads or sandwiches will give quite a flavour "lift". The dried leaves add a pleasing fragrance when incorporated into sachets, sleep pillows, sweet bags and potpourri.

Juniper
Juniperus communis

Native to the chalk and limestone regions of Britain, juniper is also widely found across Europe and from the Arctic to the mountain ranges of North Africa. Growing in North America from Massachusetts to Alaska, it also grows in the Rocky Mountains and as far south as New Mexico. It is the berries of this plant which are used and it is actually a conifer or "pine tree".

Culpeper waxed enthusiastic over the juniper, writing that the berries are a "counter-poison and a resister of pestilence, and excellent against the bites of venomous beasts ... It is a remedy against dropsy ... expels the wind and strengthens the stomach ... The berries are not ripe the first year, but continue green for two summers and one winter before they are ripe." Obviously patience is needed! To harvest the berries prior to their ripening, however, is useless.

The word "gin" is derived from the French *genévrier*, meaning juniper tree, the berries being used to flavour that well-known spirit. When used medicinally the oil of juniper is invaluable as a carminative, soporific and diuretic. A mild infusion of berries steeped in wine will stimulate the appetite. A popular Swedish beer is brewed from the berries and we are told by C. Pierpoint Johnson that a French "beer" — known as *genévrette* — is made by fermenting a decoction of equal parts of juniper berries and barley. In Lapland the bark is twisted to form a type of rope.

There are many superstitions about Juniper. For example, it was considered unlucky to dream of a juniper tree, but fortunate to dream of its berries, which foretold future success or the birth of an heir. During outbreaks of sweating sickness and plague it was thought a protection to burn juniper wood, and the smoke from Juniper fires was believed to keep off demons and evil spirits. Springs of Juniper were also hung in cowsheds to prevent cattle from being bewitched. The Welsh thought it unlucky, bringing death within the year, to fell a juniper tree. Infusions of the berry were said to restore lost youth. The ancients placed the berries on funeral pyres to protect departing spirits. It is recorded in the Old Testament that the prophet Elijah, to avoid persecution by King Ahab, took shelter under a juniper tree.

Though its area of origin is obscure, the juniper has held a favoured place for centuries.

Lad's Love
Artemisia abrotanum

This herb must have more common names than any other. It is known also as southernwood, old man, old man's love and, most interesting, maiden's ruin! This last name, no doubt, is a reference to its well known properties as a love charm. In France it is known as *garderobe* as it is an excellent moth deterrent and the silvery grey foliage dries well for use in sachets, potpourri and sleep pillows.

The species name, *abrotanum*, means "elegant" in Greek and depicts the delightful form and fragrance of lad's love.

At one time, the dried foliage and seeds of this herb were administered to children to kill worms. It was also believed that those who spoke in their sleep could be cured by adding some of the herb to wine and drinking a glass in the morning and before retiring at night. According to *Merck's Index*, a medical dictionary of 1907, lad's love was also used as a tonic and in fragrant baths and for poultices. It is recommended as a window box plant in city areas as it endures the pollution of smoke and traffic fumes better than most other plants.

Lavender
Lavendula sp.

We are told by T.W. Sanders in his *Encyclopaedia of Gardening* that lavender was introduced to Britain in 1568, but because it was such an important herb to the Romans, it is hard to believe that they did not take plants with them when they invaded England. Lavender was used to scent bath water and the name is derived from the Latin *lavare* — to wash. It is perhaps more likely that when the Roman civilisation in Britain was overthrown lavender, together with so many herbs, died out. There are many varieties of this delightfully fragrant herb. There is vera, the so-called English lavender, French and Italian lavenders, pink and white. Another variety which is the most vigorous of all is a "cross" between English and French lavenders, known as Mitcham. It is probably the hardiest, but while its silvery foliage is lovely, it does not bloom so freely as the other varieties.

Rich in history, lavender was formerly used for medicinal purposes as well as for its delightful fragrance. It was used to relieve nervous headaches and to calm hysteria. William Turner tells of it being used to wash heads "which had any deseses therein". Merck says of lavender that it is a tonic and stimulant and may be used internally and externally in hysteria, fainting, headaches, giddiness and nervous palpitation. In early times a mouthwash was made from a decoction of the flowers, and the oil was used to relieve sprains and stiff joints and was also applied to wounds. Thirteenth century Welsh physicians knew the herb as "llafant". Powdered lavender was included in many dishes as an appetite-provoking flavour and was known as a "comfort for the stomach".

The spikenard of the Bible is lavender. We read in Chapter XIV of St Mark, verses 3, 4 and 5 that, when Christ was visiting the home of a leper, "There came a woman having an alabaster box of ointment of spikenard very precious and she brake the box and poured it on His head . . . and there were some that had indignation within themselves and said 'Why was this waste of ointment made? For it might have been sold for more than

three hundred talents and given to the poor.'"

The Kabyle women of North Africa believe lavender protects them from husbandly maltreatment, while in Tuscany, Italy, it is believed to protect young children from the Evil Eye.

Until its introduction into England where it was found that lavender vera and Mitcham lavender were the hardiest varieties to grow, dry lavender flowers and young foliage were imported. It was much used for stuffing pillows and sachets and in fragrant washing waters. A conserve featuring lavender was a favourite of Queen Elizabeth I and it is said that her table always bore a pot of this delicacy.

Parkinson tells us of the white lavender: "There is a kinde hereof that beareth white flowers and somewhat broader leaves, but it is very rare and scene but in a few places with us because it is more tender and will not so well endure our cold winters."

We are told by Helen Noyes Webster in *Herbs: How to Grow Them and How to Use Them* that one should never waste a leaf or blossom of lavender. During the centuries lavender has been used for making oil of aspic to dilute delicate tones used for china painting, in varnish, as a moth deterrent spray, in herbal tobacco, snuff, and liqueurs, and to clean paint brushes. A truly versatile herb!

Lemon Grass
Cymbopogon martinii

Considered an essential herb in eastern recipes, lemon grass has long, narrow, strap-like leaves rich with true lemon fragrance when cut or torn. If tearing the leaves, however, be extremely wary as the edges are sharp.

The plant is perennial and rather hardy in all but really cold climates. It is a "thirsty" herb which requires a fair amount of water. This is natural enough as it is a native of tropical areas. Try using some finely chopped foliage over fish when steaming or baking. A little in tossed salads also adds refreshing flavour. Lemon grass is rich in vitamin A.

Lemon Verbena
Aloysia citriodora

This shrub, native to Chile and Peru, was first introduced into England in 1781 and three years later into Europe where it soon became naturalised in Italy.

The narrow light green leaves are heavily redolent with lemon fragrance and give this flavour to any drink or dish in which they are incorporated. This seems to be a herb to provoke memories as it was a favourite in many old gardens, the slightest touch being sufficient to release waves of piquant aroma. I have often incorporated sprays into floral arrangements and the resulting freshness adds delight to a stuffy room. I've also dried the leaves and used them in sachets and sleep pillows. In the latter case I have found that not only does the dried herb induce sleep but also deters mosquitoes.

Lovage
Levisticum officinale

This herb has been known as "smallage", but in the way of rustic corruption was often known as "smellage". These days it is often referred to as the "marmite" plant and the leaves, somewhat resembling

celery, have a strong yeasty flavour and fragrance. Mentioned by Pliny, it was also included in Stearne's *The American Herbal* of 1801. We are told in *The Family Herbal* of 1803 by Sir John Hill that lovage seeds "dispel wind" and that "the dried root is a soporific, and is good in fevers". Introduced by the Romans into England it quickly became a favourite pot herb. It was said that it "joyethe to growe by wayes and under the eaves of a house, it prospers in shadowy places and loves running water".

Culpeper reported: "It is a herb of the Sun under the sign Taurus." He goes on to say that "The distilled water helps the quinsy in the throat if the throat and mouth be gargled with it, and it helps the pleurisy if drank three or four times." He adds, by way of beauty hints, that the distilled water "takes away the redness and dimness of the eyes if dropped into them; it removes spots and freckles from the face".

Native to the Mediterranean countries, especially the mountainous areas of Greece, southern France and also found in the Balkans, frequently it may be found growing wild in Britain. It is not indigenous to that country, however, and it is thought that in common with so many other herbs it was an escapee from Roman gardens of long ago. It was, in fact, officially introduced to England in the fourteenth century. The Tudors and Stuarts particularly favoured it for its flavour and as a salad ingredient.

It seemed to be held in high esteem in years gone by for its medicinal qualities rather than for its value as a flavouring. It was one of the sixteen herbs that were listed in a plan of a ninth century physic garden drawn up and planted by the Benedictine monks at St Gall in Switzerland. In his *Five Hundred Pointes of Good Husbandrie* of 1573, Thomas Tusser listed lovage among those plants he considered "necessary herbs to grow in the garden of Physic".

The seed may be used in cordials and confectionery. The oil distilled from the flower and leafy top adds flavour to some tobaccos and fragrance to some perfumes.

Marjoram
Origanum majorana

Culpeper tells us that this is another herb of Mercury and "is an excellent remedy for the brain and other parts of the body". He also recommends that when dried it should be powdered, mixed with honey and used to take away "the marks of blows and bruises..." — a boon to prize fighters! He also tells us that "the juice dropped into the ears, eases the pains and singing noises in them".

We learn from T. W. Sanders in his *Encyclopaedia of Gardening* that marjoram, a native of the Mediterranean, was introduced to Britain in 1551. It quickly gained popularity and was used not only to flavour many foods, particularly cheese, eggs and sausage dishes, but when dried was used with discretion in potpourris, "sweet bags", "sweet waters" and "sweet powders". Gerard said it was "exceedingly well known to all" and listed among its virtues its ability to give relief "against the

warmbling of the stomach and [to] stayeth the desire to vomit, especially at sea".

The Greek and Romans knew and used marjoram with enthusiasm. It was traditionally used to make wreaths to crown newly-weds. It was also generally believed that a happy afterlife awaited the one who lay in a grave from which marjoram sprouted. In England sprays of marjoram and wild thyme were often placed alongside milk in dairies to prevent it being curdled by thunder.

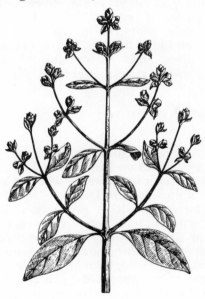

The soft rounded green-grey leaves of marjoram were used in brewing ale prior to the introduction of hops, and continued for some years after to be favoured as an aromatic flavour and preservative in beer. Marjoram tea became so favoured for its medicinal qualities as well as its pungent flavour that plants were taken to New England by the settlers where it soon naturalised itself and is now very common in the eastern states of America. Sir John Hill wrote: "The whole plant is to be used fresh; and it is best taken by way of infusion. It is good against the head ache and dizziness and all the inferior order of nervous complaints."

Italian lavender, easily distinguished by its
dark purple flower heads.

Top: Lemon verbena, a fragrant herb with many and varied uses.
Bottom: An essential ingredient in many eastern recipes, lemon grass.

Mint
Mentha sp.

There are numerous varieties of this loved and well known herb. We produce in our nursery eight different varieties, all quite distinctive. These are apple mint, eau-de-Cologne mint, pennyroyal, peppermint, pineapple mint, spearmint, basil mint and Corsican mint.

Chaucer refers to a "little path of mintes full and fenill green". It was Turner in his herbal compiled in 1568 who first referred to garden mint as "Mere Mynte". Culpeper had great faith in the efficacy of mint as a remedial herb and listed well over thirty ailments for which he recommended mint as a treatment. He tells us it is a herb of Venus and that "the juice taken in vinegar, stays bleeding, stirs up venery or bodily lust . . . applied with salt, it helps the bites of mad dogs".

The Romans introduced this herb, which is frequently mentioned in the Bible, into Britain where it quickly established itself both in gardens and in popularity. It seems that wherever civilisation spread, so did mint, in some cases becoming naturalised and invasive. It is always wise to restrict the roots of this rampant herb, particularly spearmint, eau-de-Cologne mint and peppermint varieties, by planting in containers so other herbs and plants are not overwhelmed by their enthusiastic growth.

The Greeks and Romans used mint as a bath herb to bring fresh fragrance to the water. It was also used for strewing. Mint is still used pharmaceutically and its oil is valued in cosmetics and confectionery. Apple mint has, as the name would suggest, a little apple fragrance and flavour and gives an interesting "lift" to salads and fruit cups. When dried, eau-de-Cologne mint is delightful in sachets and potpourris. It is also useful in pea or lentil dishes, giving an interesting and not easily recognised flavour. Pennyroyal is much flatter in growth habit than the other two but, like eau-de-Cologne mint, can be quite rampant, making it useful as a "binding" plant on difficult banks. Apple mint, with its dainty and charming cream and green foliage, is much less vigorous and may be used with a fair degree of impunity as a ground cover among shrubs. Pennyroyal with its fresh "peppperminty" flavour was used in ancient times to remove the staleness and purify the casks of drinking water carried on prolonged sea voyages. It is effective as an inhalant in the treatment of heavy colds and became known alternatively as the "lung mint". Formerly, crushed sprays were stored in bedding and clothes as the smell

suffocated fleas. Peppermint, with the strong flavour that gives this variety its name, is also used as an inhalant and makes an extremely refreshing tea, either hot or cold. Pineapple mint is delicately flavoured and excellent in salads and fruit drinks, as is the apple mint. A superb sauce using white wine or cider vinegar may be made from this variety and its light and pleasing flavour adds interest to roast lamb. Spearmint needs no introduction. It is probably the most commonly used herb in the world and has secured a permanent place for itself in European and Arabian kitchens. Basil mint has the flavour of both basil and spearmint.

The Corsican mint originated from the island of Corsica. It is tiny, grows only about one centimetre, yet blooms, smothering itself with almost indiscernible flowers. It is nearly impossible to see the form of these microscopic blooms with the naked eye, but in the summer months a lavender "smoke" cloud will hover over the minute deep green leaves of the herb. It is an ideal plant to use between stepping stones or for difficult areas under trees where a ground cover is wanted and turf is reluctant to grow. Growing also in Spain, this littlest of all the mints is believed to have been introduced to England about the time of the Spanish Armada. Like all mints, it does require good watering for successful growth.

There seem to be very few legends regarding mint, which is surprising for a herb with its history. It has been regarded, however, as a symbol of virtue.

In France mint is referred to as *Menthe de Notre Dame* and in Italy is known as *Erbe Santa Maria*. All varieties share in common the quality of preventing milk from curdling and so are recommended by herbalists to people on milk diets. As mint also is a great insect repelling herb, country folk in Britain were accustomed to placing sprays across doorways and along window sills to discourage flies and ants.

Mugwort
Artemisia vulgare

Known almost everywhere on the Continent as the herb of St John the Baptist, mugwort was also regarded as a source of power and protection against thunder and witchcraft. In Italy it was and in some places is still used as an augury to judge the recovery rate of invalids. When someone is ill a piece of mugwort is placed, unbeknown to the patient, under the pillow.If the sick one sleeps he is assured of a speedy recovery. If, however, he lies awake, his chances of recovery are considered very slim indeed. Mugwort was

also believed to be an effective remedy to offset fatigue brought about by travelling. The name "mugwort" is derived from the practice of using it before the advent of hops, to brew beer — "mug" being the vessel from which ale was quaffed and "wort", an early name for herbs.

The Grete Herball of 1539 tells us, "If this herbe be within a house there shall no wycked spryte abyde." In 1585 a reference was made to mugwort in an herbal Saxon manuscript.

The author, Lupton, in his *Notable Things* tells of yet another superstition relating to this herb: "It is commonly affirmed that on Midsummer Eve, there is found under the root of mugwort a coal which keeps safe from the Plague, carbuncle, lightning, and the quantan ague, them that bear the same about them ..."

It seems that medicinally mugwort was extremely useful in the treatment of gynaecological problems. Culpeper wrote that it is a herb of Venus and continued: "Its tops, leaves and flowers are full of virtue; they are aromatic and most safe and excellent in female disorders. For this purpose the flowers and bud should be put into a teapot, and boiling water poured over them, and when just cool, be drunk . . . Three drams of the powder of the dried leaves taken in wine, is a speedy and certain help for the sciatica."

Sir John Hill states: "The leaves and tops of the young shoots and flowers in this plant are all full of virtue, they are aromatic to the taste with a little sharpness. The herb has been famous from the earliest time, and Providence has placed it everywhere about our doors so that reason, and authority, as well as the notice of your senses, point it out for use, but chemistry has banished natural medicines."

Nasturtium
Tropaeolum majus

This free-flowering herb was introduced, presumably by English privateers, to English gardens in about 1596 from Peru about the time of the plunder of the Incas' gold from Peru. The gay, sun-head flowers are as edible as the "peppery" leaves. Even the seeds may be pickled for use in condiments, preserves and salads. It took several years before the nasturtium made its way across the Channel to Europe where it soon established itself. Perhaps the bright flowers represented another type of "gold" to the adventurers seeking the fabled riches of El Dorado.

Known also as Indian cress, flame flower and canary creeper, the plant we commonly know as nasturtium is in fact "tropaeolum". This name was applied to the herb as an imaginative description of the helmet-like flowers and shield-shaped leaves. It comes from the Latin *tropaeum*, a trophy. After the Greeks and Romans were victorious in battle, they displayed both helmets and shields of the defeated soldiers. The name nasturtium was applied

as the flower is so similar to that of the true nasturtiums — watercress — which are discussed later. "Nasturtium" means "nose tormentor" and refers to the "bite" of the leaves, which are delicious in salads, canapés and sandwiches. The flowers add a gay splash of colour to tossed salads.

Oregano
Oreganum vulgare

This is the stronger flavoured "brother" of marjoram. Used in many Italian dishes, it adds superb flavour to chicken and fish recipes. Gerard referred to it as "Sweet Margerome of marvellous sweet smell", while Parkinson said it was used "to please outward senses in nosegays and in windows of houses". Ibn Al Awam and Ibn Baithar, two Arabian physicians of early times, both commended oregano for its medicinal properties. The foliage of oregano contains a volatile oil which is used to alleviate rheumatism and similar complaints and when mixed with olive or some similar oil it is reputed to be useful as a cure for baldness and is effective as an embrocation when applied to bruises, sprains and strains. Veterinarians treated their animal patients with rubbing lotions of oregano and also used it as an irritant and caustic. We are told by one of the old herbalists that to smell wild marjoram frequently would ensure good health. It was used in common with many other plants as a strewing herb. Sir John Hill wrote: "Chymists sell what they call origanum but its commonly an oil made from garden thyme, it is very acrid; a drop of it put upon lint, and laid to an aching tooth, often gives ease." The two oils were often confused and we are told by C. Pierpoint Johnson writing sixty years later in 1862: "The Wild Marjoram is collected in large quantities for distillation, yielding a very strong aromatic oil, which is commonly known as Oil of Thyme, and is a very popular remedy for toothache . . ." In any case, both oils are extremely effective.

Parsley
Petroselinum sp.

There are two parsley varieties commonly available. The better known is the "triple-curled" which with its crisply twisted leaves is a superb garnishing herb. The other, Italian or continental parsley, has broader and smoother leaves. In my opinion, it is the latter which has the better flavour but both are indispensable in the kitchen. To gain maximum benefit from parsley plants it is necessary *always* to harvest the stems of foliage from the outside of the plant to enable the young growth in the centre to flourish. Remember, too, that the stems of both parslies contain more flavour and vitamins than the foliage.

It was first seriously cultivated in Great Britain in 1548 but no doubt would have been taken there much earlier by the Romans in their collections of herbs, as they knew it well. Gerard knew it as "Parsele" and wrote: "It is delightful to the taste and agreeable to the stomache", and further recommended that the roots or

seeds boiled in ale and drunk "cast forth strong venome or poyson; but the seed is the strongest part of the herbe".

Various animals enjoy it very much. Hares and rabbits will strip a planting in a very short time, and sheep thrive on pastures incorporating parsley. It is said to prevent foot rot.

In *The Grete Herball* of 1539 we are given some rather novel advice to follow when sowing parsley, which takes quite some time to germinate. However, for really crisp leaves when the parsley does ultimately emerge from the ground it is good advice: "If you will have the leaves of the parseleye grow crisped, then before the sowing of them stuffe a tennis ball with the sedes and beat the same well against the ground whereby the sedes may be a little bruised or when the parselye is well come up go over the bed with a waighty roller whereby it may so presse the leaves down or else tread the same downe under they feet."

On the other hand, to speed germination Thomas Hyll gives this advice: "To make the seedes appear more quickly steep them in vinegar and strew the bed with the ashes of bean, water with the best 'aqua vitae' and then cover the beds with a piece of woolen cloth, and the plants will begin to appear in an hour." He warns, however, that one "must take off the cloth so that they may shoot up the higher to the wonder of all beholders!"

Negroes in the southern states of America consider it unlucky to transplant parsley from the garden of an old home to a new one. On the other side of the world, some English gardeners hold that to transplant parsley would bring misfortune to every member of the household. I have never had any such woeful experience and have frequently transplanted parsley from the sun to the semi-shade it prefers.

The Greeks revered parsley as having sprung from the blood of their hero of mythology, Archimonus, known as the forerunner of death. It seems he was laid by his nurse on a parsley leaf and was eaten by serpents. Consequently when someone was gravely ill the ancient Greeks would say he was "in need of parsley". So strong was the superstition that Plutarch records a time when a marching Greek army met donkeys laden with parsley and they scattered in their fear. Considering it the herb of oblivion the Greeks made wreaths of parsley for the tombs of their dead.

Other happier uses were found for this herb which is richer in vitamin C than any other food, containing three times as much as oranges. It is also almost as rich in vitamin A is as cod liver oil. Homer tells us that warriors fed parsley leaves to their chariot horses and victors of the Isthmian games were crowned with parsley chaplets. Theocritus describes a feast:

At Sparta's Palace twenty beauteous mayds
The pride of Greece, fresh garlands
   crowned their heads
With hyacinths and twining Parsley drest
Graceful joyful Menelaus' marriage feast.

There is an old legend that where parsley grows well "Missus is Master". Parsley tea is recommended to alleviate the discomfort of rheumatism and when taken internally or applied externally will help to cleanse the skin. The leaves and stems are used to flavour all manner of savoury dishes and are a main component of the Lebanese salad, tabouleh. The herb is excellent as an adjunct to invalid food as it "perks" the appetite. In fact, no herb garden is complete without parsley.

Rose
Rosa sp.

The name "rose" comes from the Greek word, *rhoden*, meaning red, for the early blooms were of *Rosa gallica*, whose deep crimson blooms had the headiest perfume. The oldest domesticated flower on record, it had as its birthplace Persia, known today as Iran. Through traders, travellers and crusaders, it made its way through Palestine and Asia Minor to Greece. The Greeks dedicated it to

Aphrodite and made vast plantings of it in their colonies in the south of Italy in order to have plentiful supplies to satisfy the ever-increasing uses discovered for the bloom. The Oligocene deposits discovered in Colorado yielded fossilised roses estimated to be at least thirty-five million years old.

The history of civilisation can almost be charted through the history of the rose. It seems as though wherever humanity established itself, so also did it establish the rose! Drawings of roses from the sixteenth century B.C. have been discovered on the walls of caves in Knossos, Crete. Even the island of Rhodes took its name from this queen of flowers. It was often featured on coins and some dating back to 4000 B.C. have been found inscribed with this lovely flower. Specimens of rose bushes were despatched by King Sargon of Babylon (about 2637–2582 B.C.) to his capital at Akkad and we find many carvings of roses embellishing Assyrian architecture.

It is reported in the *Iliad* that Aphrodite anointed dead Hector with rose perfume, and blooms of this popular flower marked all kinds of ceremonial occasions in the capitals of ancient Greece and Rome. The rose was regarded in Rome as a symbol of the renewal of life and returning spring. As a symbol of a happy life to come, brides and grooms were crowned with chaplets woven of the flowers. The Romans used the rose and its petals to mark almost every occasion. They crowned their athletes with wreaths of the flowers and used these lovely and fragrant blooms much as confetti and ticker-tape are used in the western world today. No procession was considered complete without its shower of petals and they were strewn in banqueting halls and chambers. It is recorded that so many petals were let loose from the ceiling during a banquet arranged by Emperor Elagabalus (about A.D. 204–222) that many of those present were suffocated!

The Romans also regarded the rose as the flower of silence. There is a legend that Cupid bribed the god Harpocrates with a rose (the emblem of love) to keep silent regarding the numerous love affairs of Venus. The expression *sub rosa* comes from the Roman practice, during civil court hearings, of hanging a rose from the ceiling to indicate the need for silence and privacy. Hence, many ceilings of older buildings have a moulded rose as the centrepiece.

The rose was for so long associated with the debauchery of the Roman Empire that the early popes refused to allow the rose to be used in church decorations or at religious festivals. But as time passed this lovely and fragrant flower became the symbol of martyrdom and the five petals of the early wild roses came to represent the five wounds of Christ. The white rose was regarded as the symbol of the virginity of Mary.

It was said that St Dominic received a chaplet of roses from the Virgin Mother and it was this which came to represent the rosary. The first rosaries were formed of tiny balls made of the fragrant petals pressed tightly together.

The rose was not only universally admired and used for its beauty and perfume, but physicians found much use for the rose hip and rose petal syrups in the treatment of patients suffering from heart, liver, chest or stomach complaints. The art of distilling rose water was discovered in the tenth century by Avicenna and ancient rose perfumes such as *Oleum rosarium* were made from an oil scented with rose petals.

The damask rose is well known, and the Crusaders are often credited with bringing this eastern rose and its name back from Damascus to Western Europe. It was, however, known in France long before the Crusades so in actuality was probably brought back by very early pilgrims on their return from the Holy Land.

During the fourteenth century, Edward I adopted the rose as the emblem of England and by the fifteenth century when a thirty-year struggle took place for the crown, the conflict became known as the Wars of the Roses. The two conflicting parties were the Yorkists who chose a white rose as their badge, and the Lancastrians, who preferred a red rose. Ultimately the House of Lancaster triumphed and Henry VII was raised to the throne. On his marriage to Elizabeth of York, he chose yet a third rose to mark the peace between the two houses. Very wisely he selected a newly developed rose which provided a galaxy of blooms on the one bush – some solid pink, others pure white and some in mixed colours. It became known as the York and Lancaster rose. When the House of Tudor was in the ascendency, the deep red Tudor rose was developed and it was this variety that ultimately became the national flower of England.

There is a broad spectrum in the colour range of roses – lavender, red, pink, white, orange, yellow and, believe it or not, green! An eternal search goes on among hybridists for a blue rose, so perhaps one day that too may be produced.

There are many legends about this beautiful and fragrant bloom, several originating in England. It seems the rose is associated with Midsummer Eve when, it is believed in Somerset, a girl should enter a churchyard by moonlight, scattering rose petals. At the sound of the first stroke of midnight she must recite:

Rose leaves, rose leaves,
Rose leaves I strew,
He that will love me,
Come after me now.

Whereupon a vision of her lover would appear behind her. In neighbouring Cornwall and Devon it was believed that a girl should pick roses on Midsummer Day while the clock chimed twelve. Carefully wrapping these blooms in a sheet of white paper, the lovelorn lass should pack them away until the following Christmas Day. It augured well if the flowers were still fresh as she would then place them in her bosom, from whence the man she would later marry would snatch them. If, however, the petals had withered, the omens were poor. Traditionally a red rose was worn on 23 April — St George's Day. To dream, at any time, of red roses meant good fortune in love, but it was considered unlucky to scatter the petals from a rose which had been worn by anyone. It was also cosidered to foretell ill luck for a family if their white rose bush bloomed out of season.

Though red roses have been in demand through the centuries for cosmetics, flavouring and medicinal purposes, white roses have been preferred for the compounding of an eye-wash. Rose hip syrup, which is very rich in vitamin C, was used as a substitute for oranges for babies and young children during the Second World War in Britain, and is still valued as a source of vitamin C in many countries today.

Rose petals were used to flavour cordials and to make conserves. In Turkey they were crystallised much as we crystallise violets and were served with coffee. Only the deepest red and most fragrant were used. Try adding a few highly perfumed petals to your sugar container and serve the richly imbued crystals with coffee at your next dinner party for a new taste sensation.

There is a legend that Caliph Jehanger of Persia, walking with his new bride near rose-petal-strewn canals and fountains, noticed a fragrant oil floating on the water. This he bottled and named "Attar of Roses" (from the Persian, meaning fragrance). Thus is accounted the discovery of an important perfume component.

Rosemary
Rosmarinus officinalis and *R. prostrata*

Rosemary was first introduced into England in the 1500s, perhaps taken there by some merchantman who had visited Spain or France and who, attracted by the pungent fragrance of this shrubby herb, decided to grow it in his own garden.

Regarded as the Herb of Remembrance, we are reminded of this when we read in *Hamlet*, " There's Rosemary, that's for Remembrance."

Referred to in its lands of origin, Greece, Italy, Spain and France, as "rose of the seas" or "sea mist", rosemary has been associated through the ages with legend and folklore. In her book *The Complete Book of Herbs* Kay N. Sanecki wrote that when the Evil Woman of Etna cast her jealous invocations over the island, destroying peace and love and bringing forth mandrake, belladonna and henbane and causing them to dig their roots so deeply into the ground that only evil could come forth from the island's land, the people were in despair and the surrounding ocean became wild in its anger. The Woman of Etna had such powers that she was able to quell the sea, but a last wave crashing upon the cliffs drew a maiden into its turbulent waters and she cried, "Remember, remember". As she spoke, with her fingers grappling helplessly against the sea-wet rocks, a superb bush burst forth — the rosemary. Some authorities say the Romans introduced this herb into Britain at the time of the conquest, but others give a later date as more likely and it is believed to have become a "fixture" in the time of King Henry VIII — when it could have been among the "salats and herbs" requested by the homesick Catherine of Aragon.

Rosemary was believed to have great mystical powers, powerful enough to protect the Church, the living and the dead from all manner of evils. Grown as a matter of course in churchyards, branches were frequently used to embellish the interior of churches and it was often burned as a cheaper substitute for the more expensive incense. It was often referred to by the French as *incensier*.

Sir Thomas More lauded rosemary when he wrote: "It is the herb sacred to remembrance, and, therefore, to friendship; whence a sprig of it hath a dumb language that maketh it the chosen emblem of our funeral wakes and in our burial grounds." At funerals, a sprig of rosemary was presented to each mourner to be carried to the graveside where it was dropped on the coffin. At weddings, as an emblem of fidelity, rosemary freshened with perfumed waters was woven into the chaplets worn by brides.

In 1607, the Reverend Roger Hacket had published his sermon *A Marriage Present*. In it he stated: "Speaking of the powers of Rosemary, it over-toppeth all the flowers in the garden, boasting man's rule. It helpeth the brain, strengtheneth the memories, and is very medicinable for the head. Another property of the Rosemary is, it affects the heart. Let this Rosmarinus, this flower of men, ensigne of your wisdom, love and loyaltie, be carried not only in your hands, but in your hearts and heads."

No festivity seemed complete without rosemary in some form or another. A few leaves would be finely chopped for inclusion in both Christmas puddings and wedding cakes.

Another piece of folklore is in *Bankes Herbal* where we are instructed to "make thee a box of the wood of Rosemary and smell it and it shall preserve thy youth".

A herb that has been long associated in legend with the Virgin Mary and Christ, rosemary is believed to have almost miraculous powers. It is traditionally carried, with other herbs, in the processions of the Lord Mayor of London as a preventative against plague.

In Elizabethan times, when a rosemary bush matured the thickened stem would be cut and used in the manufacture of the lovely lutes which provided so much of the music traditional to that era. At wedding feasts in Tudor England friends of the bride would make a nosegay of sprigs of the herb bound with gold silken threads or lace (known as "bride lace") and hand it to the bridegroom to ensure his fidelity. A ballad of 1543 tells of a wedding at which "there was a fair bride-cup of silver gilt carried before her [the bride] wherein was a goodly bunch of Rosemary . . . hung about with silken ribbons of all colours".

Roses cover a pergola as part of a herbal walk in an
Australian garden planted for fragrance.

Top: Prostrate winter savory.
Bottom: The yellow button flowers of santolina
light up any garden.

Rosemary has long been associated with the head, be it for headache, remembrance or, as in many Mediterranean countries, a hair tonic. It is frequently brewed into an infusion to be used after shampooing as a final rinse, which it is believed will forestall the appearance of grey hairs!

In some countries it is distributed on a certain day to be worn in memory of the fallen of two world wars.

Sir John Hill in his *The Family Herbal* wrote that a conserve of rosemary may be made "by beating up the fresh gathered tops with three times their weight in sugar". He also gives the recipe for Hungary Water which was reputed to have cured Elizabeth of Hungary of her dropsy. "The famous Hungary Water is made also of these flowery tops of Rosemary. Put two pound of them into a common still, with two gallons of melasses spirit, and distil off one gallon and a pint. This is Hungary Water."

Culpeper writes that "the decoction of Rosemary in wine helps the cold distillations of rheum into the eyes and other cold diseases of the head and brain, as the giddiness and swimmings therein . . ."

Judging by the number of romantic superstitions attributed to rosemary, particularly in Great Britain, this fragrant herb could be of the heart as well as the head! Margaret Baker in her *Discovering the Folklore of Plants* says it was considered to bloom at midnight on Twelfth Night. Used as a protection against spirits, fairies, lightning, injury, and to promote success in business enterprises, it was also believed to be an infallible love charm. In Derbyshire a girl would put a crooked sixpence and a sprig of rosemary under her pillow in order to dream of her future husband. On 20 January — St Agnes' Day or Eve — a more elaborate procedure was followed. A sprig each of rosemary and thyme would be sprinkled with water. At nightfall the sprigs would be placed in a pair of shoes, which were then put either side of a maiden's bed with the plea: "St Agnes that's to lovers kind,

Come, ease the trouble of my mind", whereupon a vision of her future husband would appear. In another county a girl would place a dish of flour on Midsummer Eve under a rosemary bush and the following morning would find her future husband's initials written in it.

Rosemary was said to cure bad dreams when placed under the bed and a comb of rosemary wood cured baldness. It was also believed that to drink from a spoon of rosemary wood was an insurance against poisoning. In cooking rosemary goes splendidly with lamb and veal and adds a delicious flavour to tomatoes.

Rue
Ruta graveolens

This blue-grey very pungent herb is of the citrus fruit family, Rutaceae. Native to southern Europe, it has been known for centuries. In Pliny's day it was prescribed for eighty-four different ailments. According to him, artists ate rue in great quantities. Credited not only with preserving sight, sharpening vision and easing tired and strained eyes, it was also believed to give second sight. Like most other herbs it had its share of superstitions and the Greeks regarded it as a mystical herb able to give great protection against enchantments and magic spells. Rue was thought to relieve the nervous indigestion which at times inflicts itself upon shy dinner guests. This particular problem was seriously attributed to witchcraft or evil wishing by some malicious fellow diner!

Culpeper advised rue for the treatment of sciatica and joint pains, recommending that the latter be "anointed" with it. He also recommended it for "the shaking fits of ague, to take a draught before the fit comes". He had a rather novel prescription for relieving earache and aiding failing sight: "The juice thereof warmed in a pomegranate shell or rind, and dropped into ears, helps the pains of them. The juice of it and fennel, with a little honey, and the gall of a cock put thereunto, helps dimness of the eyesight."

The King of Pontus, Eupator Mithridates (A.D. 120-63), who ruled from 120 to 63 B.C., was a toxicologist who devised a remarkable poison antidote in which rue was the main ingredient. The generic name *Ruta* is derived from a Greek word meaning "to set free" and was given to this herb because of its property of releasing one from many maladies. Mithridates experimented personally with so many poisons and antidotes over such a long period that when defeated by Pompey, he tried in vain to poison himself, but on discovering his immunity he persuaded a slave to stab him to death!

Grown commonly for domestic medical remedies in Britain and on the Continent, rue was also valued as a mystical protective herb against evil and wrongdoing by witches. It was used, too, as a disinfectant against plague. A rumour erupted in London in July 1760 that an outbreak of this dreaded pestilence had been discovered at St Thomas' Hospital.

As a result, the price of rue and wormwood skyrocketed and by the next morning had risen by forty per cent at Covent Garden. The hospital's medical staff, to avoid panic, were forced to issue an official denial. Gerard tells us that "the leaves of Rue eaten with the kernels of walnuts or figs stamped together and made into a masse or paste, is good against all eville aires, the pestilence or plague."

Rue symbolised both repentance and sorrow. It was used variously to help, bless, curse or harm. It was also believed to be medicinally safe if gathered early in the day but poisonous if picked later. Among other ailments, rue was used to treat dog bite and there is a case on record that at Cathorpe, Lincolnshire, rue was used with dramatic success to cure the whole town of the bites of a mad dog which had run amok, attacking the population. Believed to prevent people talking in their sleep, it was thought that rue would grow better if stolen. Rue tea will kill fleas and, it was said, shot boiled in rue water always found its mark. As a strewing herb against pestilence, it was used to combat jail fever. Judges always carried rue with other herbs into court as a protection against infections.

It is of little culinary value but occasionally a few finely chopped leaves are added to Italian salads.

A tisane may be made of the fresh leaves but much sweetening is required to disguise the bitter flavour. The aroma is extremely pungent and penetrating.

Sage
Salvia sp.

The Latin proverb "Why should a man die whilst sage grows in his garden?" indicates the high regard in which this herb was held as a health-giver. The Latin belief in "Sage the Saviour" was endorsed by people in many countries. Native to the Mediterranean area it was used in numerous prescriptions for all kinds of maladies, as a tooth whitener, a hair-colour restorer and a strewing herb. Strongly favoured as a flavouring, no garden was considered complete without at least one sage bush.

Dioscorides believed it to be the remedy for almost all kidney ailments and he claimed that while curing these problems, it turned grey hair black. He also recommended it for rheumatism, ulcers, consumption, coughs and sore throats. Pliny believed it would cure snake bites. Gerard described sage as a herb of the brain and memory and since earliest times it has been used to counteract the processes of declining faculties and weakening memory.

Extremely effective as a digestive aid, sage is used extensively in those countries where oil is important in the preparation of food, and also in pork or other dishes featuring rich meats. It is added to egg and cheese dishes and leaves are sometimes added to beer during the brewing, resulting in a delicious herbal beer. In Jamaica a cooling drink is made from fourteen grams of dried sage leaves combined with the juice of a lime and a spoonful of honey. This mixture is poured into a litre of boiling water and allowed to stand for thirty minutes before straining for use. It is taken as a treatment against the delirium of fevers.

Sage is a flavouring in the preparation of Derby sage cheese which takes on a delightful marbled green appearance. The tang of the sage lessens the richness of the cheese. The leaves may also be "fired" to deodorise a sick room.

It was believed that sage would alleviate grief and a common practice was to scatter sage leaves, which wither slowly, or to plant sage bushes, on graves. Samuel Pepys wrote in his diary: "Between Gosport and Southampton we observed a little churchyard where it was customary to sow all the graves with sage." The plants were considered so valuable that for a period it was the custom to plant rue nearby to protect them from "noxious" toads.

The most aromatic sage grows on the Greek islands near Fiume and there, since the golden days of ancient Greek civilisation, a superb "sage honey" has been produced which is considered a great luxury.

As well as the more familiar grey-leafed sage, there is now available a pineapple-flavoured form, *Salvia rutans*, which is delicious in tossed salads and fruit cups as well as rich meat and cheese dishes.

Many legends are attached to sage. Considered a symbol of domestic virtue it was believed that "If the Sage tree thrives and grows, The Master's not Master and he knows." It was thought that the herb grew best for the wise. As a barometer of health, sage flourished in a garden where the master of the house enjoyed good health and began to wither if he fell ill. Sage was considered rejuvenating and was often eaten between slices of bread and butter as a sandwich.

As a remedy for ague, sufferers ate

seven leaves of sage on seven mornings before breakfast. John Evelyn wrote of sage: "It is a plant indeed with so many and wonderful properties that the assiduous use of it is said to render men immortal."

In Northamptonshire a girl would pick, without damaging the bush, twelve sage leaves at midnight on Christmas Eve in the hope of seeing the shadowy form of her future husband. In Lincolnshire the same ritual was followed on St Mark's Eve, while in Staffordshire girls went into their gardens at midnight on All Hallows' Eve and gathered one leaf at each stroke of the hour. It seems that girls were more anxious to glimpse their future spouses than were lads!

Santolina
Santolina chamaecyparissus

Often called the "cotton lavender", santolina is in fact no relation to the lavender family at all. It is, however, an exquisite little herb. Its foliage is pure silver and gives an impression of "knotting". Its flower is in the form of miniature yellow buttons and the whole is a joy in a sunny spot in the garden. We are told by Helen Noyes Webster in *Herbs: How to Grow Them and How to Use Them* that santolina was highly favoured as a border for "knot gardens".

The flower is used medicinally as a treatment for ringworm and as a general vermifuge for the expulsion of worms from both humans and animals. The American settlers used the fragrant foliage as a moth deterrent and an oil is extracted from stem and leaf for use in compounding some perfumes. It dries well for use in sachets or potpourri and is charming when incorporated in posies or floral arrangements. It was rarely used in herb gardens except as a decorative feature and yet its pungent fragrance makes it a natural protector of leafy crops from white moth attack. Sprigs may be used to flavour beef stock and roast pork.

Savory
Satureia sp.

There are three types of savory cultivated. Winter savory (*Satureia montana*) has a hot, biting flavour. Prostrate winter savory (*S. repandens*) has somewhat similar flavour and makes a superb basket subject as it flowers freely in autumn, its pure white blooms cascading like sea foam over the narrow dark green foliage. Summer savory (*S. hortensis*) is the only annual in the group and unlike the other two genus members has pale pink summer flowers. It is much softer to the touch than either of its relatives. The savories are among the herbs that have been used since early times and Virgil advised planting specimens adjacent to bee hives to give an interesting and pleasing flavour to the honey.

The ancients believed that the savories belonged to the satyrs and it is not difficult to imagine the foliage of winter savory being fashioned, with its deep green sharply pointed leaves, into crowns for these woodland deities. The ancient Romans favoured a savory sauce mixed with vinegar as a dressing for fish and meat dishes, much as we use mint sauce.

Introduced from Europe into Britain in about 1562, the savories quickly gained favour and established a firm place in herb usage. T. W. Sanders in his *Encyclopaedia of Gardening* recommends that winter and prostrate winter savory should be replaced every fourth year as they become rather woody.

Shakespeare in *The Winter's Tale* includes savory in Perdita's posy along with hot lavender, mints, and marjoram, of which she remarked, "These are flowers of middle summer and, I think, they are given to men of middle age."

Culpeper favoured the herb and preferred the summer savory to the evergreen varieties for drying and described it as being "both hotter and drier than the winter kind". I have found the reverse to be true and favour winter savory. Much could depend on climate, however, as this has a significant effect on the strength of herb flavours. Culpeper also recommended that the juice of savory should be heated with oil of roses and dripped into the ears to alleviate singing noises and deafness.

Parkinson writing of winter savory said it was dried, powdered and mixed with fine breadcrumbs "to breade their meate, be it fish or flesh, to give it a quicker relish". It was considered the perfect herb with which to season trout. It was also used for veal and turkey stuffings and to flavour pork pies and sausages. It was dried in the still room for potpourri, sachets and washing waters. The savories were, in fact, so popular that people emigrating to various countries took with them seeds and cuttings of these appetising herbs to add flavour to food in their new lands.

Savory is also useful as a treatment against flatulence and colic. In common with most of the other herbs, a tea may be made by using one teaspoon of leaves to a cup of boiling water and infusing for five minutes before straining and drinking. Never use milk with herbal teas and if sweetening is required, use honey rather than sugar.

Tansy
Tanacetum vulgare

This delightful herb is found over a widespread area, its fronds of dark feathery green fern-like foliage adding charm to any herb garden. Preferring a moister spot than most herbs, tansy thrives along river banks. Paxton in his *Horticultural Register* of 1833 writes of having seen it "growing plentifully" on the banks of the River Derwent and along the banks of numerous other rivers and streams. An inhabitant of water places, hedgerows and roadsides, it is a plant which does need confining in similar fashion to mint as it likes to travel. It is, however, a splendid "tub" plant and I have often used a pot of tansy near our

barbecue area to deter flying insects, which it does admirably.

Occasionally made into tea, tansy was also used to flavour puddings, particularly at Easter, when the juice was incorporated into the mixture: "On Easter Sunday is the pudding seen, To which the Tansy lends her sober green." In Sussex it was believed that tansy leaves placed in shoes would prevent an attack of ague. Tansy was used also among the bitter herbs which the Israelites used to consume with their Paschal lamb. For centuries tansy was valued medicinally for several maladies including wounds of various kinds and disorders of the kidneys and womb. Taken internally by those women seeking abortion, it was also used externally by those desiring children. Hot fomentations of tansy leaves were applied to sprains and areas affected by rheumatic or arthritic pain.

Like so many herbs it was taken by settlers leaving their homelands to establish themselves in new countries. In America, for example, it quickly naturalised itself in the eastern states.

The name tansy is derived from the Greek *athanasia*, meaning immortality. It was given this name by Pliny and was considered immortal because of the long life of its little buttons of yellow blooms. A friend of mine found that by including fronds of tansy in her floral arrangements the life of the flowers filling the vase was considerably lengthened. It was also discovered that, when preparing corpses for burial and herbs and flowers were included in the shrouds or coffins, tansy helped to preserve the bodies.

The foliage has a delightful fragrance which was best described by the Dutch physician Boerhaave when he affirmed: "This balsamic plant may well supply the place of nutmegs and cinnamon, for I believe that Asia does not supply a plant of greater fragrance than the Tansy."

Tarragon
Artemisia dracunculus

This is a herb which is unique in that there are no legends attached to it. It has been used medicinally and we are told by Sir John Hill in his *The Family Herbal* of 1803 that "an infusion of the fresh tops works by urine and gently promotes the menses".

There are two types available, Russian and French tarragon, the latter having the superior flavour. This also is one herb that does not dry well as most of the volatile oil is lost in the drying process. It should always be cut fresh when needed for the kitchen.

The French tarragon is a much smaller plant than the Russian, which is a Siberian wild herb. The former is native to southern Europe and parts of Asia. Its narrow, slightly incised leaves are a rich green and taste vaguely like aniseed. The leaves of Russian tarragon are eaten in Iran as an appetiser. The French tarragon is used to flavour various sauces, fish and chicken dishes. At one time the herb was considered a cure for toothache and an aphrodisiac!

Tarragon is related to such herbs as mugwort, lad's love and wormwood — all members of the *Artemisia* family — and its name comes from the Greek *drakon* — a serpent — from an old belief that it was an infallible cure against the bites of venomous insects or snakes.

Thyme
Thymus sp.

A herb popular since ancient times, thyme has been used for centuries, not only for flavouring, but also for medicinal and fumigatory purposes.

There are many types that will grow in the herb garden or with great effect throughout the general garden. One charming variety, known as Shakespeare's thyme, will quickly smother a bank or mound to form a herb seat — superb to rest on during a warm afternoon. Another one or two bring delightful fragrance when placed between stepping stones and accidentally bruisd. Both will stand a little traffic. One is the "woolly thyme" or *Thymus languinosa*. The soft velvety grey-green foliage releases a sweet perfume and carries occasional pale pink flowers, while the other, *T. nitidus*, is crisp to the touch and exhudes a warm "spicy" aroma. It is embellished by masses of cheery pink blooms.

Others, more useful to the kitchen, have a range of flavours. The one most commonly known is the garden thyme (*T. vulgaris*). Its familiar zesty flavour and fragrance have been used for centuries to flavour all manner of soups, stews, meat and poultry dishes. Its leaves are short, narrow and somewhat sharply defined at the tip. Turkey thyme (*T. westmoreland*) has been a favourite of chefs for seasoning all poultry dishes and its leaves are somewhat blunter in appearance and of a softer green than those of the garden thyme. Lemon thyme (*T. citriodorus*) is a special favourite of mine. The slightly rounded deep green tiny glossy leaves are redolent with the flavour and fragrance of fresh lemons as the name would indicate. I use it in tossed salads, fish and chicken dishes and with vegetables such as carrots, zucchini and beans. On every occasion it adds a superb and interesting flavour. Silver posy (*T. argentus*) is a pet. It forms low mounds of silver and green with its short narrow silver-edged leaves and crowns itself with dainty pink flowers as do most other culinary thymes. The flavour is somewhat milder than that of the garden thyme so it is ideal to use for just a breath of flavour. Caraway (*T. herba-barona*) is the most trailing of the culinary herbs, with the flavour suggested by its name. Excellent in baskets, it carries

drifts of deep magenta blooms in summer.

There are many legends about thyme. Associated with death, it was used as a fumigant after sacrifice and at funerals and was frequently planted on Welsh graves. Those belonging to the Order of Oddfellows carry sprigs at

funerals and these are tossed into the open grave of a deceased member. In England thyme was associated particularly with murdered men and the souls of the dead were believed to dwell in the sweetly perfumed flowers of the herb. The aroma of thyme is said to linger about a path near Dronfield in Derbyshire where a young man murdered his sweetheart.

Thyme was beloved by fairies and in the Ashmolean Library, Oxford, there is a seventeenth century recipe for a potion "To enable one to see the Fairies".

Bees love to linger over thyme blooms and as the Greeks considered this herb an emblem of courage, Lancastrian ladies frequently embroidered a bee hovering over thyme on scarves that they gave to their favoured knights. The various members of the thyme family "joy to be placed in a sunny and open place". Combined with dried rosemary, dried thyme together with freshly ground cloves makes a splendid moth repellent and clothes freshener, worth remembering when storing winter woollens and furs for the summer months.

Francis Bacon enjoyed the fragrance of thyme in his garden and directed the planting of paths with many herbs but with emphasis being placed on thymes, so that when trodden they would perfume the air "most delightfully".

Medicinally, thyme was found to be very valuable. Sir John Hill wrote: "A tea made of the fresh tops of Thyme, is good in asthmas and the stuffings of the lungs: it is recommended against nervous complaints; but for the purpose the wild Thyme called mother of Thyme is preferable. There is an oil made of Thyme that cures the tooth-ache, a drop or two of it being put upon lint and applied to the tooth." Mother of thyme is botanically *T. serypyllum*. In *The Useful Plants of Great Britain*(1862), C. Pierpoint Johnson wrote: "In France a decoction of the plant has been successfully used to cure the itch, and some other skin disorders. Linnaeus recommends it for relieving headache caused by 'the effects of intoxication' . . . There can be no doubt that to this and other aromatic herbs much of the superiority of flavour in the flesh of sheep, fed upon down land, is due; for though many have denied that these animals ever eat these strongly flavoured plants the fact is perfectly well known to all who have had an opportunity of observing them feeding on hill pastures, where the Thyme and

Marjoram abound, those herbs always being cropped close when growing with grass." Thyme is a remarkable and versatile herb and an essential one for both garden and kitchen.

Violet
Viola odorata

Beloved by ancient Greeks and Romans, the shy and charming violet was cultivated for use in kitchen and still room where the herbal medicines, lotions and potions were compounded.

Culpeper said: "It is a fine pleasing plant of Venus, of mild nature and no way hurtful." Indeed, it was regarded as the ancient flower of love and was chosen by the Greeks as the flower of Aphrodite.

Top left: Tansy effectively deters flying insects.

Top right: Elderberry — its leaves, berries, bark and flowers are all useful.

Bottom left: Wormwood, prized for its magnificent silver foliage.

Bottom right: The feathery foliage of yarrow.

Lemon thyme has many delightful culinary uses.

They called it *Ione* because Jupiter, fearing the vengeful jealousy of Juno, changed his beloved Io into a white heifer and created violets for her to feed upon. Shakespeare had a fondness for violets and mentions them in *The Winter's Tale* and *Hamlet*.

This lovely and fragrant flower has numerous legends attached to it as do so many herbs. The English considered it unlucky to have just a few violets in the house, and it was believed that a small number would have an adverse effect on hens. Dreams of violets foretold an improvement in fortune but to see one blooming in autumn augured death or an epidemic. In Gloucestershire the people believed violets harboured fleas. The ancient Romans thought that a wreath of violets about the neck or a chaplet worn on the head prevented drunkenness. Napoleon loved the flower, which reminded him of his boyhood in the Corsican woods. His followers adopted the violet as their emblem, and Napoleon claimed he would return from exile "with the violets in the spring". He plucked violets from the grave of Josephine who had worn them to her wedding with Bonaparte. It was found after he died in 1821 that he had placed the violets in a locket which he wore about his neck. Unlike most other herbs, violets do not retain their perfume after drying nor their original colour.

There is an old English sonnet in which the following lines appear: " Violet is for faithfulnesse, Which in me shall abide", and an Eastern proverb tells us: " The excellence of the Violet is as the excellence of El Islam above all other religions."

John Evelyn in his *Acetaria* of 1699 writes: " Violet Leaves, at the entrance of spring fried brownish and eaten with Orange or Lemon Juice and Sugar is one of the most agreeable of all the herbaceous dishes."

The Persians and Romans brewed violet wine, which they esteemed highly. They also used the leaves in salads and made violet conserves. Cosmetically this lovely flower was also found to be useful.

The Romans used it for perfume and to add fragrance to creams and lotions. Tons of violets were produced at Paestum to answer the needs of the wealthy Mediterranean communities. The Britons of ancient times also used violet cosmetics and would steep flowers in goat's milk to keep their ladies' complexions fair.

Medicinally the violet was used extensively. We are told in a tenth century herbal: "For them that may not slepe for sickness seeth this herb in water and at even let him soke well hys fiete in the water to the ancles, wha he goeth to bed, bind of this herbe to his temples."

Culpeper described its many medicinal virtues and further suggested poultices of the leaves for reducing inflamed swellings. Violets were also used to relieve the inflammation of the lungs and chest.

Sir John Hill tells us: "The flowers are the part used, boiling water is to be poured upon them just enough to cover them, and it is to stand all night; when it is strained clear off, the sugar is added to it, at the rate of two pounds to each pint, and it is to be melted over the fire, this makes a syrup of violets an excellent gentle purge for children."

Watercress
Nasturtium officinale

This is a herb native to Great Britain and is found along all kinds of waterways, hence its name. A true nasturtium, it is also found in other parts of the world.

Robert Henrick in the seventeenth century wrote a poem "A Thanksgiving to God for His House", in which he said:

Lord, I confess too when I dine
The Pulse is Thine,
And all those other Bits, that bee
There plac'd by Thee;
The Worts, the Purslain, and the Messe of
Watercresse
Which of Thy Kindness Thou has sent;
And my content.

A flourishing trade in watercress began in England about 1808. Always in season, it is high in vitamin C and iron content and is an ideal salad herb. Watercress sandwiches have long been a favourite at English garden and afternoon tea parties and it makes a most agreeable garnish. Wherever the English migrated they took with them supplies of watercress and, in fact, it grew so well in New Zealand that it has come to be regarded there as a weed! It was introduced into America very early. Provision of fresh foods was made in various ways for passengers and crews of the sixteenth century ships and it was believed that later "cabin" passengers took supplies of watercress with them across the Atlantic, maintaining it in a jar of water.

Pliny gave this herb its generic name of *Nasturtium* which comes from *nasus* — nose, and *tortus*, twisted, probably in reference to the fact that the hot, peppery taste causes a contraction of nasal and mouth muscles. Pliny also noted that watercress was used for the treatment of brain disorders. Among the ancient Greeks it was highly esteemed as a salad herb, and also as a dietetic medicine. There was a saying which roughly translates into "eat cress" and which was applied to those whose wits were believed to have deserted them. Xenophon recommended that the Persians give it to their children to increase their strength and stature.

It is believed that a Nicholas Meissner of Erfurt, Germany, was the first man to cultivate watercress commercially in Europe and this proved so successful that shortly after it was grown on this basis in both Holland and Germany. C. Pierpoint Johnson reported that in the early nineteenth century in England upwards of 6000 bunches were daily sent to market! Obviously it was very popular. Gerard, rather quaintly, recommended that the leaves be used by young girls to keep their complexions fair.

Wormwood
Artemisia absinthium

This lovely silver-foliaged plant is silky to the touch and provides a delightful accent in the garden. Growing well in a tub, it could be used with great effect on a patio, and as it deters flying insects it would be a good idea to use a plant near an entrance for this purpose.

This herb belongs to the *Artemisia* genus and is kin to tarragon, mugwort and lad's love. One theory is that it was used by Artemisia, Queen of Carea, who in honour of the plant's medicinal value gave it her name. Pliny on the other hand attributed the discovery of the herb to the goddess Artemis. The ancients held it in high regard as a diuretic and tonic, a digestion aid and appetite restorer. It was considered a sure antidote against seasickness and many vegetable poisons. Greek and Roman physicians also administered it as a vermifuge.

The English herbalist Tusser, writing in 1557, referred to wormwood's use as a strewing herb:

> While Wormwood hath seed get a handful or twaine,
> To save against March, to make the flea refraine.
> Where chamber is sweeped and Wormwood strowne,
> No flea for his life, dare abide to be knowne.
> What saver is better, if physick be true,
> For places infected than Wormwood and Rue.
> It is as a comfort, for hart and the braine,
> And therefore to have it, it is not in vaine.

In Wales the herb was frequently used instead of hops to flavour beer. A similar brew called Wermuth beer was made in Germany and the French liqueur absinthe has this herb as its main flavouring ingredient. It is rarely used in the kitchen and most medical use has passed from general practice. Used over-enthusiastically, wormwood can act as an irritant and cause giddiness and headache.

Yarrow
Achillea millefolium

Favoured for use in divination for spells and witchcraft, yarrow was also known as "devil's rattle" and "devil's plaything". We read in Halliwell's *Popular Rhymes* that an ounce of yarrow sewed up in flannel and placed under a pillow with the following words,

> Thou pretty herb of Venus tree,
> Thy true name it is Yarrow
> Now who my bosom friend must be
> Pray tell thou me tomorrow

would surely do just that! In Sussex it was believed that yarrow must be picked from the grave of a young man, in the western counties it had to be harvested at full moon, and in Herefordshire, to be effective, it had to be picked from a churchyard

unfamiliar to the enquirer. If girls cut the stem of yarrow crossways the cross section would reveal the initials of their future husband.

We learn from an old herbal that "the leaves being put into the nose do cause it to bleed, and easeth the pain of the megrim". Consequently, one of the old names applied to the herb was "nose-bleed".

It was believed that yarrow strewn on the hearth would deter witches and that if worn on the person or tied to the cradle, it would protect a baby. Hung up on the eve of St John, it kept sickness away for the year ahead. Custom decreed that a bridal couple should eat it at their wedding to ensure their love continuing for at least seven years. In the Hebrides, to gain second sight, a yarrow leaf was held against the eye.

Thought to possess some narcotic properties, in Germany yarrow was used early in the nineteenth century as a tonic medicine. The Swedes placed it in beer to increase the intoxicating qualities and to keep the beer from souring.

Native to the whole of Europe, it has been introduced to Australia, New Zealand and North America. It is the herb that Chiron the centaur introduced to Achilles in order that he could make a salve of it to heal his wounds at the battle of Troy.

Culpeper wrote that "it stays the shedding of the hair, the head being bathed with the decoction of it". A French legend refers to it as the *herbe aux charpentier* for they said it was "good to rejoyne and soundre woundes". A tisane to be sweetened with honey may be made from the young leaves.

PROPAGATING HERBS
3

Though some herbs may be grown from seed, most should be grown from root division or cuttings. Some herbs such as mint and oregano do not have a true flavour when raised from seed. With other herbs such as wormwood, rosemary and lavender, seed germination and subsequent growth are very slow. In the case of the lavender family, seed of some of its members is not freely obtainable.

It is possible to make a miniature propagating "house" with a seedling tray or plastic pot. Using skewers or paddle-pop sticks, form a "fence" around the perimeter of the chosen container and when the cuttings or root divisions have been inserted or the seeds sown, stretch plastic film over the top of the sticks and tuck under the base of tray or pot. Seed-raising mix is available from your local nursery and this is an ideal medium to use for propagation. With bay trees great patience is required as even under the ideal conditions provided by modern nurseries, the cuttings of this herb take months to form roots. Hormone powder, also obtainable from the retail nursery, may be used for faster root formation, but it is rather expensive.

Tip cuttings are exactly that! Take a piece about 3 cm long, or for wormwood, bay, lavenders, lemon verbena, elder and perfumed geraniums, about 6 or 7 cm long, from the tip of sprays or branches and *gently* strip the leaves for about two-thirds of the cuttings and insert in the seed-raising mix. If hormone powder is used, dip the cutting into it before inserting in the seed-raising mix. If sowing seeds, just barely cover them with sand and firm lightly with a trowel or fingers.

HERB	LIFE EXPECTANCY	PROPAGATION METHOD	TIME OF YEAR
Angelica	Biennial	Seed — must be very fresh	Spring through to autumn
Balm	Perennial	Seed or cuttings	All year for cuttings. Spring and summer for seeds
Basil (all varieties)	Annual	Seed preferably, though tip cuttings may also be taken	Mid-spring to mid-summer for seed sowing. Cuttings may be taken through early summer
Bay	Perennial	Cuttings only	All year
Bergamot	Perennial	Cuttings or root division. Seed if available	Cuttings during summer. Root division during winter and early spring. Seed in spring
Borage	Annual	Seeds only. This herb self-sows readily	From early spring through to late summer

HERBS FOR THE HOME AND GARDEN

HERB	LIFE EXPECTANCY	PROPAGATION METHOD	TIME OF YEAR
Burnet, salad	Biennial	Seeds only	Spring through summer
Calendula	Annual	Seeds only	Late summer for autumn and winter flowering
Camomile	Perennial	Root division or seed	Year round
Caraway	Annual	Seeds only	Spring through to autumn
Carnation	Biennial	Seeds or cuttings	All year for cuttings. Seed in spring
Chervil	Biennial	Seeds only	Most of the year but *not* during mid-winter.
Chives	Perennial	Seeds or clump division	Clumps must be divided in autumn. Seeds may be sown throughout the year.
Coriander	Annual	Seeds only	Through very early spring to late summer
Dandelion	Annual	Seeds only	Through very early spring to late summer
Dill	Annual	Seeds only	Late winter to late summer
Elder	Perennial	Cuttings only	Year round even when deciduous
Fennel	Annual	Seeds only	All year, except in winter
Garlic	Biennial	Corm (small bulblet)	All year
Geranium	Perennial	Seeds *may* come true of perfumed varieties. Cuttings are preferable	All year, except in late winter

PROPAGATING HERBS

HERB	LIFE EXPECTANCY	PROPAGATION METHOD	TIME OF YEAR
Horehound	Perennial	Seeds or cuttings — preferably cuttings	All year
Horseradish	Perennial	Root division	Warmer months — tends to go underground in cooler weather
Hyssop	Perennial	Seeds or cuttings	Cuttings in late summer; seeds in early spring through to late summer
Juniper	Perennial	Cuttings only	During mid-summer
Lad's love	Perennial	Cuttings only	All year
Lavender	Perennial	Cuttings preferable, though seed is available of *L. vera*	Late summer to mid-winter
Lemon Grass	Perennial	Root division only	Late spring to late summer. In mild climates, early autumn as well
Lemon verbena	Perennial	Cuttings	All year, even when deciduous
Lovage	Perennial	Seeds only	Early spring to late summer
Marjoram	Perennial in warm climates or situations. Annual under cooler conditions	Seeds or cuttings	Very late winter through to mid-summer
Mint (all varieties)	Perennial	Cuttings or root division. Some varieties not available in seed, but flavour is better in all varieties from cuttings or root division	All year. Faster root formation in warmer months

HERB	LIFE EXPECTANCY	PROPAGATION METHOD	TIME OF YEAR
Mugwort	Perennial	Cuttings preferable. Seed is difficult to obtain	All year, but as with mint, roots develop more readily in warmer months
Nasturtium	Perennial	Seeds, though cuttings are also viable	Warmer months are preferable, though all year germination is possible
Oregano	Perennial	*Cuttings only.* Seed-grown plants have very little, if any, flavour	All year, though warmer months preferable. Flowering tips are unsuitable
Parsley (both varieties)	Biennial	Seeds only	All year
Rose	Perennial	Possible from cuttings but it is recommended that established plants be purchased as growth is stronger	During late winter or spring
Rosemary — prostrate and upright	Perennial	Seeds or cuttings. Cuttings are preferred as resulting plants have better flavour	From early spring to early winter for cuttings and spring to summer for seeds
Rue	Perennial	Seeds are slow to germinate but give better results than do cuttings	All year except mid- to late winter
Sage (both varieties)	Perennial	Seeds are not commercially available for pineapple sage, but seeds of common sage or cuttings of both are recommended	All year
Santolina	Perennial	Cuttings only	All year
Savory, winter and prostrate winter	Perennial	Cuttings only	During warmer months as growth diminishes during cool weather

PROPAGATING HERBS

HERB	LIFE EXPECTANCY	PROPAGATION METHOD	TIME OF YEAR
Savory, summer	Annual	Seeds only	Very late winter through to mid-summer
Tansy	Perennial	Cuttings or root division	All year, preferably in warmer months as it diminishes in growth during cooler months
Tarragon	Perennial	Cuttings or root division	During late spring to late summer. Disappears underground during winter
Thyme (all varieties)	Perennial	Seeds when available, or cuttings	All year, but cuttings strike better during warmer months
Violet	Perennial	Cuttings, root division or seeds	Spring through to summer. Violets also self-sow seeds
Watercress	Perennial	Seeds or cuttings	Seeds should be sown through spring and summer. Cuttings may be taken in autumn
Wormwood	Perennial	Cuttings	All year
Yarrow	Perennial	Root division	All year

HERB PRODUCTION CHART
4

I n the following chart, annual means plants which, almost always grown from seed, have a brief season of a few months; biennial describes those plants which live for two years, usually having stronger pungency and flavour at the commencement of the second year; perennial means those plants which live for many years and benefit from light judicious pruning.

HERB	LIFE SPAN	SOIL PREFERRED	SITUATION	SOWING ADVICE
Angelica	Biennial	Rich, and medium moisture content	Shaded	Sow *fresh* seed about 2 cm deep throughout summer
Balm	Perennial	Moist, warm and fairly rich	Sheltered and sunny	Seed may be sown all year in temperate climates
Basil (sweet and bush)	Annual	Well drained but moist	Sheltered and sunny	Seed in early spring after last frosts
Bay	Evergreen perennial tree	Moderate quality	Sheltered, full sun	—
Bergamot	Perennial	Rich, moist	Sunny or semi-shaded	—
Borage	Annual	Almost any	Sunny	Shallow sowing of seed between early spring and late summer
Burnet, salad	Perennial	Chalky	Sunny	Late spring and early summer
Calendula ("pot" or English marigold)	Annual	Well drained	Sunny	Shallow sowing of seeds during spring, or seedlings
Camomile	Perennial	Dry	Sunny or semi-shade	—
Caraway	Annual	Well drained	Sunny	Seed in early spring through to early autumn
Carnation	Perennial	Well drained	Sunny	Seeds or tip cuttings
Chervil	Biennial	Sandy and well-drained	Semi-shaded in summer, full sun in winter. Ideal under deciduous trees	Any time. However, if planted in late summer, will crop in autumn

HERB PRODUCTION CHART

PLANTING GUIDE	FLOWERING	HARVESTING FOR DRYING	PARTS GENERALLY USED
Transplant young seedlings in autumn	Usually second year in spring	Leaves prior to flowering and throughout summer. Dig roots the first year in autumn	Flowering stalks, leaves and roots for candying, potpourris and bread making respectively
Seed, division or tip cuttings spring and autumn	Summer	Early summer to early autumn	Whole or chopped leaves in salads and teas
Plant seed in intended growing area	Late summer	Mid-summer, just before flowering	Leaves only in sauces and salads
Autumn — cuttings. Protect from winter frosts	—	All year round	Leaves only for most casseroles
Division late spring and summer	Summer	Before flowering, early to late spring	Leaves and flowers separately for salads and teas
—	Mid-spring until heavy frosts	Young leaves only at any time	Tender young leaves and flowers separately for soup and casseroles
Thin seedlings out to 15 cm apart	Summer	Just prior to flowering	Leaves in salads and sandwiches
—	Late autumn to late winter	—	—
Division and cuttings in early spring	Late winter to early autumn	Flowers throughout summer	Flowers, foliage rarely as a tea and in beauty products
Set out seedlings when of reasonable size	Early summer to late autumn	Seeds after flowers are spent	Seeds, foliage mainly as a garnish
Add a little lime to well worked soil	Cuttings all year, seeds in warmer months	—	Flowers only with white parts removed
—	Mid- to late summer in second year	Prior to flowering	Foliage only used in herbal health care as well as having a wide range of culinary uses

HERBS FOR THE HOME AND GARDEN

HERB	LIFE SPAN	SOIL PREFERRED	SITUATION	SOWING ADVICE
Chives (onion or garlic)	Perennial	Almost any	Warm and semi-shaded	Spring
Coriander	Annual	Almost any	Sunny	All year except winter
Dandelion	Perennial	Any	All situations except full shade	Spring
Dill	Annual	Not too light, but well drained	Sunny	Early spring to early autumn
Elder	Perennial deciduous shrub	Damp and rich	Sunny	—
Fennel	Annual	Well composted and rich	Warm and sunny	Early spring to early autumn when frosts have finished
Garlic	Perennial	Very rich	Sunny and damp	—
Geranium	Perennial — not hardy	Light and sandy but rich in compost	Sheltered and warm	—
Horehound	Perennial	Average but well drained	Sunny	Seed, in spring through to late summer
Horseradish	Perennial	Rich and moist	Damp — needs room to spread	—
Hyssop	Evergreen shrub	Light — well drained	Sunny	About 6 mm deep
Juniper	Evergreen shrub	Chalky or with lime worked in well	Sunny	—

HERB PRODUCTION CHART

PLANTING GUIDE	FLOWERING	HARVESTING FOR DRYING	PARTS GENERALLY USED
Divide in autumn	Remove blooms summer to mid-autumn. Will drain goodness from herb	When about 23 cm in height	Foliage only to flavour dairy products and vegetables
Set out seedlings when large enough	Summer — mid-autumn	When seed is ripe	Seeds mainly. Foliage called "Chinese parsley" and used in Oriental dishes
–	Spring to autumn. Best if flowers are nipped off	Spring to autumn. Select only young leaves, and roots	Roots and young leaves only especially in salads and casseroles
–	Summer	Foliage before flowering. Seeds when flowers are spent	Leaves and seeds have many culinary uses
Cuttings in autumn; root division	Summer	Flowers mid- to late summer. Berries in autumn	Berries and flowers in teas and other drinks
–	–	–	Foliage and swollen stem base — an aniseed-flavoured addition to salads and sauces
Most of year, except during late winter	Remove flowers which appear just prior to the foliage dying off	All year. Lift bulbs when leaves are yellow — before winter if wishing to dry	Bulbs. *Young* foliage may be used also in salads and sandwiches
Cuttings in autumn under glass	Early summer until early autumn	From mid-autumn or before first frost	Leaves in potpourris and in some cooking
Divide plants regularly	Early summer to early autumn	Any time	All parts. Excellent in tea, beer and candy
Early spring and autumn by piece of root	–	Nine months after planting dig up roots	Roots mainly, but young leaves add zest to salads
Spring and autumn	Mid-spring to late summer	Possible to cut both before and after flowering	Flowers and young tender tips of foliage
Cuttings in late summer	Mid- to late summer	Autumn. Store only for twelve months	Berries, but must be ripened black

HERBS FOR THE HOME AND GARDEN

HERB	LIFE SPAN	SOIL PREFERRED	SITUATION	SOWING ADVICE
Lad's love	Perennial	Well drained	Sunny	Cuttings only
Lavenders (all varieties)	Perennial	Well drained with a little lime worked in	Sunny	*L. vera* may be grown from seed, others from cuttings
Lemon grass	Perennial	Moist. This is a plant of the tropics	Sunny	Root division only. Unrooted pieces may be "struck" under plastic or glass
Lemon verbena	Perennial but frost tender. Will perform well as a house plant in a well lit room. Deciduous if grown outdoors in a temperate climate	Well drained. A little compost or peat moss added to light soil is ideal	Sunny	Cuttings only when well rooted
Lovage	Perennial	Any rich soil	Damp. Sunny or semi-shade	Spring or autumn
Marjoram	Annual in cool areas	Reasonably rich	Warm and well drained	Mid-spring to late summer
Mint (apple)	Perennial	Moist and rich	Best in sun but will accept semi-shade	—
Mint (Corsican)	Perennial	Moist and rich	Semi-shade	—
Mint (eau-de-Cologne)	Perennial	Moist and rich	Best in sun but will accept semi-shade	—

HERB PRODUCTION CHART

PLANTING GUIDE	FLOWERING	HARVESTING FOR DRYING	PARTS GENERALLY USED
When danger of frosts has passed plant well rooted cuttings	Rarely	During warm months when oil content is at peak	Foliage may be dried and used in sachets for moth repulsion
When danger of frosts has passed *L. vera* seedlings may be set out. Well rooted cuttings of all varieties may be planted	Late spring to very early autumn	Flowers and leaves during warm months when oil content peaks	Both flowers and leaves carry delightful fragrance and may be dried for use in sachets and potpourris
In cold climates this must be protected from frost	–	Mid- to late summer	Foliage used in Oriental dishes and as a tea
Although this is a deciduous shrub, protection should be given from frosts	Summer	Any time during warm weather	Foliage. Flowers rarely. Used as a repellent and in teas, drinks and salads. Excellent among cut flower arrangements as a room deodoriser
Seed or division spring and autumn	Mid- to late summer	Several cuts possible from late summer to late autumn	Leaves, stalks and seeds good in vegetarian dishes and as a tea
–	Mid-summer to early autumn	It is possible to cut twice – late April and late May	Leaves and flower buds
Cuttings in spring or root division in autumn	Summer	Not suitable – too soft	Leaves – ideal in mint sauce
Divisions of plant with roots all year except cooler months	Summer	–	None
Cuttings in spring or root division in autumn	Summer	As for spearmint	Leaves for potpourri, flower arrangements (flowers may also be used here), added to bath water, in citrus drinks and jellies and with steamed peas

HERBS FOR THE HOME AND GARDEN

HERB	LIFE SPAN	SOIL PREFERRED	SITUATION	SOWING ADVICE
Mint (penny-royal)	Perennial	Moist and rich	Best in sun but will accept semi-shade	—
Mint (peppermint)	Perennial	Moist and rich	Best in sun but will accept semi-shade	—
Mint (pineapple)	Perennial	Moist and rich	Best in sun but will accept semi-shade	—
Mint (spearmint)	Perennial	Moist and rich	Best in sun but will accept semi-shade	—
Mint (variegated apple)	Perennial	Moist and rich	Best in sun but will accept semi-shade	—
Mugwort	Perennial	Any	Grows wild in any position	—
Nasturtium	Annual	Sandy. For better flowering keep soil poor. Leaves prefer richer soil	Sunny	Throughout spring and early autumn
Oregano	Perennial	Chalky or gravelly	Warm, dry and well drained	Spring and autumn
Parsley (triplecurled and Italian)	Biennial	Rich, well worked	Partial shade	Mid-winter to mid-autumn
Rose	Shrub (deciduous)	Clay soil	Sunny	—
Rosemary (upright and prostrate)	Perennial; evergreen shrub	Light, sandy, even chalky	Sunny aspect — best against wall	Mid-summer for seed
Rue	Hardy evergreen shrub	Well drained light soil — grows well in tubs	Dry, sunny	Seed during summer

HERB PRODUCTION CHART

PLANTING GUIDE	FLOWERING	HARVESTING FOR DRYING	PARTS GENERALLY USED
Cuttings in spring or root division in autumn	Summer	Not suitable — too soft	Leaves for flea repulsion and when steaming new potatoes
Cuttings in spring or root division in autumn	Summer	One cut first year, two afterwards	Leaves in tea, fondants and lime jelly
Cuttings in spring or root division in autumn	Summer	Not suitable — too soft	Leaves in mint sauce or in salads and fruit drinks
Cuttings in spring or root division in autumn	Summer	Prior to flowering in summer and then again in early spring	Leaves for garnishing and flavouring in salads, etc.
Cuttings in spring or root division in autumn	Summer	Not suitable — too soft	Leaves in sauces, drinks and when steaming peas
Division or tip cuttings in warm months	Mid-summer to early autumn	When buds are formed but not open	Buds only in tea
—	Almost all year	Leaves prior to and after flowering	Leaves and flowers. Seeds may be pickled as caper substitute
Cuttings spring to autumn (preferable to sowing seed as flavour is better)	Mid-summer to early autumn	Prior to flowering	Leaves mainly; occasionally flowers
—	Second year	Best in summer or autumn	Leaves and stems. The latter are very rich in vitamin C
Autumn. Cuttings when pruning — late spring or late autumn	From mid-spring	While flowering	Flowers and rose hips
Tip cuttings in late autumn.	Early summer to early autumn	Any time after late spring flowering. Upright rosemary more suitable	Leaves in tea or leaves and flowers separately for flavouring
Tip cuttings in late winter under glass	Mid- and late summer	Any time up to early summer. Good pruning of established plants in late summer will encourage new leafy growth	Flowers used in eye lotion. Leaves used in tea to relieve abnormal blood pressure. Foliage may also be mixed in poultry mash to prevent croup in flocks

HERB	LIFE SPAN	SOIL PREFERRED	SITUATION	SOWING ADVICE
Sage (grey-leafed and pineapple flavoured)	Perennial	Light, dry, chalky	Dry and sunny	Seed in late spring and early summer
Santolina	Perennial	Well drained	Sunny	Summer
Savory (winter, prostrate winter, and summer)	Winter and prostrate — perennial. Summer savory is an annual	Poor, very well drained. Prostrate variety best over banks, etc.	Full sun	Seeds for summer savory between late spring and mid-summer
Tansy	Perennial	Well drained	Sunny	—
Tarragon (French)	Perennial but herbaceous. Goes under-ground dur-ing cold weather	Well drained and light. Will even accept poor soil	Dry and sunny	—
Tarragon (Russian)	Perennial, more vigor-ous than French	Well drained and light. Will even accept poor soil	Dry and sunny	Seeds during late spring to late winter
Thyme (all varieties)	Perennial evergreen shrublet	Chalky, light and well drained	Prefers hot, dry and sunny	Spring
Violet	Perennial	Well worked, slightly damp	Sun or semi-shade	Mid-winter, but first-quality seed must be selected
Watercress	Perennial	Damp	Prefers semi-shade	Seeds all year
Wormwood	Perennial	Light and dry	Light semi-shade. Grows well in con-tainers	Seed very slow to germinate
Yarrow	Perennial	Dry to mod-erately rich	Sun	Seed slow to germinate

HERB PRODUCTION CHART

PLANTING GUIDE	FLOWERING	HARVESTING FOR DRYING	PARTS GENERALLY USED
Cuttings from early spring and throughout summer	Narrow-leafed variety blooms in late summer	Cut between early and mid-autumn	Leaves as a flavouring for fish and poultry as well as a tea
Tip cuttings between early spring and early winter	Between early summer and early autumn	After flowering	Leaves — primarily dried for use in moth-repellent sachets
Cuttings or division spring until late autumn	Summer	Prior to and after flowering. Summer savory is not suitable for drying	Leaves of all types for soups and stews
Cuttings or divisions through warm months	Summer	Not normally dried	Leaves. Flowers used in floral arrangements
Division spring and summer, or tip cuttings. Mark plants with stake or rock as it will, when herbaceous, travel up to 60 cm underground	French tarragon does not flower	Cut wherever new shoots are of sufficient length — usually between late spring and early autumn	Leaves to flavour sauces or vinegar
Division spring or summer, or tip cuttings	Summer	Cut wherever new shoots are of sufficient length — usually between late spring and early autumn	Leaves. Russian has inferior flavour to French
Division or tip cuttings early spring to late autumn	Mid- to late summer	Before and during flowering period	Leaves and blooms
Cuttings or division in summer	Early and mid-spring and again in early and mid-autumn	During flowering period	Principally flowers. Leaves, however, were formerly used medicinally
Divisions in warmer months	—	—	Leaves in salads
Tip cuttings early spring to late autumn	Late summer	Throughout the year	Leaves dried and used in potpourris and sachets. Tea as slimming aid, otherwise rarely used in the kitchen
Root division autumn and spring	Throughout late spring and summer	Throughout the year	Flowers useful in floral arrangements. Leaves used to staunch bleeding

PRACTICAL HERB USES
5

Many times I have been asked for simple hints on herb use. A favourite question is, "What herb goes with what food?" To answer this I have drawn up the following list, and have also prepared a chart, showing how herbs may be used to keep a garden and household healthier. So often commercial insecticides are used in garden and house, yet herbs are nature's own insecticides and do not pollute the atmosphere. Several herbs benefit other plants and so should be "companion planted" for healthier crops. These are also included in the chart.

What herb goes with what food?

FOOD	HERB
Beef	basil, bay, garlic, horse-radish, oregano, rosemary
Cakes and desserts	carnation, coriander seeds, marigold, apple mint, lemon balm, lemon verbena, scented geraniums, violets
Cheese	dill, chives, nasturtium, sage, parsley
Drinks	borage, burnet, lemon balm, lemon verbena, mints, scented geraniums, rosemary
Eggs	chervil, chives, dill, fennel, parsley, tarragon
Fish	bay, dill, lemon balm, lemon thyme, lemon verbena, sage, salad burnet, lemon grass
Lamb	dill, garlic, marjoram, mint (sauce), oregano, rosemary, thyme (all varieties)
Pork	garlic, marjoram, rosemary, sage, thyme (all varieties)
Poultry	bay, lemon balm, lemon verbena, lovage, marjoram, oregano, parsley, rosemary, sage, tarragon, lemon or turkey thyme
Salads	basil, burnet, chervil, chives, dandelion, garlic, dill, marigold, marjoram, mint (*not* eau-de-Cologne), nasturtium, parsley, tarragon, thyme, lemon grass, watercress
Shellfish	basil, chervil, dill, lemon balm, lemon verbena, parsley, thyme (lemon), tarragon, horseradish
Soups	basil, bay, chervil, chives, dill, lovage, marjoram, oregano, parsley, thyme (all varieties)
Stews and casseroles	bay, chives, lovage, marjoram, oregano, parsley, thyme (all varieties), watercress

VEGETABLES

Beans	Any savory, but preferably winter or prostrate
Cabbage family	Caraway seed, dill foliage or seed
Carrots	Thymes
Cauliflower	Dill foliage or seed
Cucumber	Dill foliage or seed
Mushrooms	Thymes

Onions	Dill foliage or seed, thymes
Parsnip	Dill foliage or seed
Peas	Mints
Potatoes	Chives, dill, parsley (either Italian or triple-curled or spearmint)
Pumpkin	Chives, parsley (either Italian or triple- curled)
Squash family	Savories or thymes
Tomatoes	Basil, oregano, rosemary (upright or prostrate)

(See the following chapter for recipes.)

Preserving Herbs

By freezing or drying or, with basil, keeping in water or oil, it is possible to have a supply of herbs from the summer garden available through the winter months, though there are many herbs which, because they lose much of their volatile oils and flavour when dried, are best used fresh, or frozen in ice cubes. Examples are parsley, chervil, lemon balm, the various mints, fennel, lovage and tarragon. These herbs will dry quite well but their flavour is better when fresh.

Drying

Herbs such as marjoram, oregano, thyme and other "woody" herbs may be cut just prior to blooming. Take the required amount of foliage before the sun is upon the plant, bunch the stems and hang them upside down in an airy, well-ventilated room. Alternatively, the sprays may be laid separately on a biscuit tray in a *very* mild heat in the oven. If using the oven method, it is wise to dry each variety separately in order that the various aromas do not intrude upon each other. When the foliage is quite dry, rub it from the stems and pack into opaque jars or wooden boxes. Though clear glass jars have eye appeal, they are unsatisfactory for herb storage as the light diminishes the strength of the herb.

Drying flowers is somewhat different to the process used in drying foliage. Pick the flowers early in the morning before the sun has had a chance to burn them. Have ready a fine mesh screen or old sheet and spread the flowers in a single layer upon this. Store in a dry shady spot to dry. Very moderate to low oven heat may be used, but the colour of naturally dried flowers is superior to the colour of those dried by artificial heat. Keep each variety separate, ready for inclusion in teas, sachets, and so on.

Freezing

There are two ways to freeze herbs. The first and simpler method is to place leaves of the chosen herb into the compartments of ice cube trays, fill with water and freeze. Store the cubes in a clearly labelled plastic bag. These cubes may be dropped into soups, stews or casseroles to provide garden fresh flavour. Alternatively, cut sprigs of herbs, wash, pat dry and wrap in foil parcels. Individual herbs or bunches of mixed herbs may be used. Label all packets for easier identification and place in the freezer until required.

Preserving Basil

As well as by freezing and drying, basil can be preserved by two other methods. Sprays of fresh basil leaves survive for quite a long time in a container of water. In fact, I have known basil to grow roots in the water, which should be changed daily. Merely snip off the required amount of foliage for use. Mint may also be treated this way.

The alternative method with basil is to store in oil. Pluck as many basil leaves as possible and wash well. Pat dry gently to avoid bruising and pack in a clean glass jar. Fill with good quality olive oil and store in the refrigerator. To use, merely lift the required number of leaves from the oil. When all the basil has been used the remaining oil, which will have a distinct flavour of the herb, may be used in oil and vinegar dressing.

Herb Use Chart

HERB	COMPANION PLANT	GARDENING/PET CARE
Angelica	Stinging nettle improves the oil content by up to 80% when planted nearby.	Blooms attract bees to the garden.
Balm	Small plantings benefit all vegetable crops.	Lemon balm will promote flow of milk in cows. Rub inside of hives with a handful of lemon balm and the bees will never quit the hive.
Basil	Plant near tomatoes to counteract fruit fly and to improve the quality of the fruit.	Helps to repel flying insects. Do not plant near rue.
Bay	—	—
Bergamot	—	Blooms attract bees to the garden.
Borage	Plant adjacent to strawberries in order to achieve heavier cropping.	Blooms attract bees to the garden.
Burnet, salad	—	Excellent sheep and cattle fodder, particularly on chalky soils. May be interplanted with Dutch clover.
Calendula	Plant with roses to control nematode worms. Also aids in controlling white fly in tomatoes.	Blooms attract bees to the garden and plants keep ground healthy.
Camomile	Small plantings nearby increase the strength of peppermint flavour in that mint. Planted among wheat in ratio of 1 camomile per 100 wheat plants, promotes heavier and fuller ears. Plant one plant camomile to every 4 m of onions for better cropping.	Known as "the plants' physician", camomile keeps the garden healthy and repels flies and midges — very useful when incorporated into compost heaps.
Caraway	Ideal as a companion plant with peas. Do not plant near fennel.	Beneficial to plant in heavy soils as it will assist it to become crumbly.
Carnation	—	Blooms attract bees to the garden.
Chervil	Radishes grown near chervil have a hotter flavour.	Grow in semi- shade for best results.

PRACTICAL HERB USES

COOKING	HEALTH
Roots and stems counteract tartness in rhubarb, etc.	Leaves used in bath to stimulate the skin. Tea useful as a digestive aid.
Leaves add "lemony" flavour to desserts, cakes, fruit and vegetable salads and drinks.	Lemon balm tea has an anti-spasmodic effect, stimulates the heart and calms the nervous system. Balm tea makes a good lotion for "problem" skins.
Used in all tomato and savoury Italian dishes. Also with cheese and new potatoes.	May be taken as a laxative or used to counteract gastric cramp.
Leaves flavour soups, stews, milk puddings, game , poultry, etc.	Oil of bay used to relieve insect stings. Also oil is used in toilet preparations.
Blooms and leaves added to salads and fruit cup.	Tea used to induce sleep.
Young leaves may be torn into salads or cooked as spinach substitute. Flowers used to decorate cakes, fruit cup, etc. May be candied.	Borage tea may be taken as a mild diuretic.
Leaves give light cucumber flavour to salads and sandwiches. Added to soups at the start of cooking time they will enhance other herb and vegetable flavours.	Salad burnet tea acts as a mild stimulant.
Marigold petals may be added to salads for piquancy. May also be used as a saffron substitute.	Marigold ointment aids in healing ulcers and wounds.
Flowers used to enrich sherry flavour. Also useful as a garnish.	Camomile steam baths useful in treatment of acne. Compresses of the herb encased in tissues or soft cloth are helpful in reducing eye inflammation.
The seeds make heavy bread and cake more digestible. Also delicious in soups and cheese dishes.	Caraway tea aids the digestion.
Petals used to flavour wine and also in salads.	Carnation cordial or tea is sometimes used to reduce fever. Dried petals used in potpourri.
Chervil finely chopped into salads, mayonnaise, egg dishes, sauces and soups imparts a delicately delicious flavour.	Leaves have blood cleansing and diuretic qualities. Finely chopped and warmed chervil relieves the discomfort of bruises and painful joints when applied to area of discomfort.

HERB	COMPANION PLANT	GARDENING/PET CARE
Chives	Chives planted under apple trees prevent attack by apple scab. Also will assist to keep roses free from aphis and benefit carrots when planted nearby.	Chives tea will assist in combating powdery and downy mildew on gooseberries, cucumbers and marrows.
Comfrey	–	Excellent addition to diet of cattle, particularly cows. Assists in strengthening legs of horses, especially riding or racing types.
Coriander	Must not be grown near fennel, but assists growth and formation of anise plants.	Attracts bees and other beneficial insects to the garden when in bloom.
Dandelion	Benefits alfalfa when planted nearby.	Blooms attract bees to the garden.
Dill	Do not plant near carrots. Small quantities beneficial when planted among cabbages and corn.	Dill assists in repelling cabbage moth. The blooms are most appealing to honey bees.
Elder	–	Attracts birds to the garden. When planted around compost heaps it assists in fermentation. Bruised leaves heaped under fruit trees will aid in repelling green fly or aphis.
Fennel	Do not plant near dwarf beans, tomatoes, kohlrabi or caraway.	Blooms attract bees to the garden. Helps to repel fleas. Rub into pets' fur and plant near kennels or cat baskets.
Garlic	Do not plant near peas or beans. Garlic and roses mutually benefit each other. Garlic will help to promote the growth of vetch.	Garlic tea is a useful control against late blight on tomatoes and potatoes. Is also effective against brown rot of stone fruits.
Geranium (scented)	–	Leaves placed among the bedding of pets will help as an insecticide. Blooms attract bees to the garden.
Horehound	–	Leaves will ward off flies. Blooms attract bees to the garden.
Horseradish	Plant in corners of potato plots to benefit potatoes.	Horseradish tea made from young leaves is effective against brown rot.
Hyssop	Grape vines give heavier yields when hyssop is planted nearby. Do not plant near radishes.	Hyssop tea is effective against plant diseases caused by bacteria. Blooms attract white cabbage moth, luring it away from the crops.

PRACTICAL HERB USE

COOKING	HEALTH
Give light onion flavour to all savoury dishes and salads.	Chives stimulate the appetite and so are indispensable in invalid cooking. Also act as a mild antibiotic.
Young leaves are excellent when lightly steamed and served as a vegetable.	Considered an excellent healing herb for open wounds and also as a "bone setter". Comfrey tea assists in relieving chest conditions.
Crushed seeds are used in the preparation of curry powder and for flavouring pickles and apple pie.	Coriander tea is useful as a carminative. In mediterranean countries the leaves when used as a pot herb are believed to be an aphrodisiac.
Young leaves excellent in salads and sandwiches. Crushed seed may be brewed into a herbal "coffee".	Is considered helpful to the function of the gall bladder. Also is an excellent blood cleanser and diuretic.
Use seed or foliage to render cabbage, cauliflower and cucumber more digestible. Seeds also excellent in cheese dishes.	Tea brewed from seeds or foliage aids in relieving flatulence or stomach cramp.
Flowers used in tea and fritters. Berries may be added to wine or sauce. Flowers will also flavour jams and jellies.	Flowers made into tea act as diuretic and blood purifying agents. Elderberry juice is helpful for winter colds and sciatica discomfort. Cold elderberry tea acts as good skin-toning agent.
Use with fish dishes. Swollen stems may be served in salads or steamed as a vegetable.	Fennel tea is excellent as an eyewash. It also aids in slimming programmes.
Use with discretion in dressings, soups, stews, casseroles and salads.	Used as a cleansing and antiseptic agent and is very rich in iodine.
Use leaves in fruit punches and in the preparation of sweets and cakes.	Dried leaves useful in potpourri to cleanse rooms of disagreeable odours. Some varieties possess styptic qualities.
Leaves used in candy, tea, syrup and beer brewing.	Dried leaves useful as a snuff to clear nasal congestion. Horehound candy efficacious in treatment of bronchitis. Horehound tea is also effective in chest conditions.
Root used in shellfish cocktails. Young leaves may be torn into salads. Grated root also used in sauce for roast beef.	Strongly diuretic, stimulates appetite and aids digestion.
Young leaves give "minty" flavour to vegetable and fruit salads and fruit cup. Also add interest to fruit pies.	Hyssop flower tea relieves catarrh and is a stimulant. Also acts as a diuretic.

HERBS FOR THE HOME AND GARDEN

HERB	COMPANION PLANTING	GARDENING/PET CARE
Lad's love	Plant adjacent to fruit trees for for cleaner and healthier fruit.	Helps to repel cabbage moth.
Lavender	–	Repels all types of moth.
Lemon Grass	–	–
Lemon verbena	–	Foliage deters midges and other flying insects.
Lovage	Improves vegetable crops when planted nearby.	Blooms attract bees to the garden.
Marjoram	Helps keep vegetable garden healthy.	Repels flying insects. When fed to pregnant cows marjoram will prevent abortion. Marjoram and balm tea helps cows to regain strength after calving.
Mint (all varieties)	Grow adjacent to cabbage bed to help keep plants clean from cabbage grub.	Repels ants and helps to control aphis. Rub peppermint or spearmint on exposed skin when gardening to keep flies away. Pennyroyal repels fleas so rub into the fur of pets.
Mugwort	–	Blooms attract bees to the garden.
Nasturtium	Plant near broccoli to keep clean from aphis. Also repels woolly aphis from apple trees when plants are grown around trees. This herb will aid radishes, too, as well as potatoes.	Helps repel ants and generally keep the garden healthy.
Oregano	Assists in repelling the cucumber beetle and aids all other vegetables.	Blooms attract bees to the garden.
Pansy	A few plants among the rye crop will improve the yield.	Blooms attract bees to the garden.
Parsley	Parsley planted among roses and tomatoes is extremely beneficial.	Sick goldfish will improve if a handful of parsley is placed in their water. Blooms bring honey bees to the garden.
Rose	Roses have mutual beneficial effects on parsley, garlic, lupins and mignonette.	Blooms attract bees to the garden.

PRACTICAL HERB USES

COOKING	HEALTH
–	Dry for use in potpourri as air freshener. Also useful in sachets as moth deterrent.
Use leaves and blooms to flavour oil and vinegars for salads.	Dried or fresh flowers will exhude oil into hot baths, which is beneficial to the skin.
Chopped leaves are added to oriental dishes.	Tea rich in vitamin A.
Use leaves whenever a strong lemon flavour is required, e.g. in drinks, tea, fruit or vegetable salad.	Tea soothes tension headaches and eases taut nerves.
Leaves add "meaty" zest to vegetarian dishes. Also add good flavour to sandwiches. Seeds are used to top loaves, etc.	Lovage tea stimulates the digestive system and is a good diuretic. The seeds stimulate the appetite.
Use in sausages and egg dishes, tomato and vegetable juices and with chicken and lamb.	Equal parts of marjoram and balm make a healing tea. Marjoram contains disinfectant qualities. Try using the tea as a mouth wash. Oil of marjoram good for rubbing into sprains and bruises.
Spearmint used in mint sauce, and with new potatoes and in fruit cup. Eau-de-Cologne mint used in steaming peas and in citrus drinks and jellies. Apple mint and pineapple mint good in fruit or tossed salads. Peppermint makes a refreshing tea and flavours fondants.	Oil of peppermint used medicinally. Mint possesses good cleaning qualities as a furniture polish. Spearmint tea helps to relieve head and toothache.
Flower shoots when in bud are used to flavour duck, pork or fat dishes.	Flower shoot tea helps relieve the pain of rheumatism, digestive problems, and chronic diarrhoea.
Leaves used in sandwiches and salads. Flowers are also tasty in vegetable salads.	A strong antibiotic. Leaves carry high quantities of vitamin C and have diuretic qualities. Nasturtium also makes a good pepper substitute.
Leaves add delicious flavour to Italian and fish dishes, stews, etc.	Oregano tea is considered helpful as a gargle for sore throats and as a mouthwash for infected gums.
–	Dried flowers used in potpourri to cleanse stale room odours.
Use as a flavouring ingredient in all savoury dishes and soups and as a garnish.	Parsley tea is excellent in treatment of kidney problems and is a good diuretic. Cold tea assists in removing freckles. Chew Italian parsley after eating garlic.
Petals may be crystallised and served with coffee or used in tossed or fruit salads. Rose hips may be pureed as a sauce.	Rose hip tea is an excellent diuretic and aids kidney and bladder. Rose petals, when dried, are an essential ingredient in potpourri.

HERB	COMPANION PLANTING	GARDENING/PET CARE
Rosemary	Rosemary and sage are mutually beneficial. Plants of rosemary will repel the carrot root fly. (Prostrate rosemary is equally effective in all areas.)	Assists in repelling flying insect pests.
Rue	Do not grow near basil.	Repels house and stable flies. A little rubbed into the fur of pets will help to repel fleas.
Sage	Do not grow near cucumber seedlings. Sage does benefit cauliflower and cabbage plants, deterring white cabbage moth and rendering the vegetable more digestible.	Generally assists in keeping the garden free of harmful flying insects.
Santolina	–	Helps to repel flying insects.
Savory	Aids the growth and development of onions and green beans.	Honey bees enjoy the flowers.
Tansy	Plant adjacent to peach trees to promote healthier and cleaner fruit.	Will repel flies, ants and moths. Also controls worms in horses.
Tarragon	Benefits the garden generally.	–
Thymes (all varieties)	Plant adjacent to cabbage to repel root fly.	Bees enjoy thyme blooms. Thyme honey is considered a delicacy.
Violet	Violets will inhibit germination of wheat.	Blooms attract bees to the garden.
Watercress	Infusion of watercress leaves aids raspberries.	–
Wormwood	Do not plant near fennel, sage or caraway.	Repels most flying insects, including flea beetle and cabbage moth.
Yarrow	Yarrow has a beneficial effect on all herbs and vegetables.	Rye grass and yarrow grown together provide an excellent pasture for cows. Use in compost heaps.

PRACTICAL HERB USES

COOKING	HEALTH
Use with discretion in meat, chicken, and vegetable dishes. Is good with small boiled onions. May also be added to fruit and claret cups.	Rosemary wine stimulates the heart. Tea is also good for flatulence and neuralgic pains. Rosemary water is good facial wash to benefit the skin.
–	Rue tea is useful in combating dizziness and female disorders.
Use in pork and fatty fish or poultry dishes.	Sage tea is an excellent gargle for inflamed throats. Sage tea is an excellent digestive. Dried leaves may be burnt in a sick room as a defumigant.
Sprigs may be used in pork dishes and will render the meat more digestible.	–
Use in cooked beans and bean salads, soups, stews, etc.	Useful as a pepper substitute for those with stomach ulcers.
Leaves used in milk or tansy puddings.	Compresses of leaves assist grazes to heal quickly.
Used in béarnaise sauce and vinegar and with chicken.	Useful to settle an upset stomach. Take as tea.
Use in soups, stew, casseroles. Lemon thyme delicious in salads and fish dishes. Most thymes are delicious with poultry.	Lemon thyme is used in potpourri. Thyme tea is a useful sedative and tranquiliser.
Flowers may be crystallised or used to garnish fruit cups or salads.	Violet tea is a sedative. The leaves are useful for poultices to soothe and heal wounds.
Use leaves as a garnish or in soup; sandwiches.	Leaves boiled in water help clear spotty skin. Infusion soaked on pad and laid on forehead relieves headaches.
–	Flowers and leaves crushed together may be brewed into a tea for weight loss.
–	Yarrow has styptic qualities and quickly heals wounds. Tea relieves fatigue.

Herbal Sprays

Herbal sprays are easily made and provide pollution-free ways of controlling both disease and pests in the garden. The leaves or shoots being gathered for the sprays must be collected early in the morning, no later than ten o'clock, and before the plant comes into bloom. If gathered while a plant is in flower, the leaves will not have so much strength. Younger plants are better than older ones for providing leaves with volatile oils. Dry in the shade and store, for preference in tin boxes. The exceptions to the rule of foliage only are yarrow and camomile, where the flowers are the parts used.

Making a herbal solution for spraying is somewhat different to making herbal teas for drinking. For a spray, place the leaves (about one good handful) in a pot and cover with water. Bring it just to boiling heat and remove it from the stove. Dilute it with four parts of water, and stir for ten minutes. Use immediately.

Horseradish tea is useful to combat brown rot (*Sclerotina fructigena*) a common blight on apple trees. Choose young leaves and use the spray at first signs of attack.

Other useful herbs for sprays are sage, wormwood, nasturtium, camomile, yarrow and chives. For the pest they will combat, refer to the companion planting and gardening sections of the preceding chart. To make sure the spray adheres, add about half a cupful of diluted clay.

Chives spray will overcome apple scab, but the process of brewing the mixture is a little different to earlier instructions. Do not bring to the boil, but rather pour the boiling water over the dried herb and infuse for fifteen minutes. Dilute this mixture with twice the amount of water used for the tea and stir. This spray is also effective against gooseberry mildew.

Camomile tea is effective against damping off in cold frames and greenhouses, and is a useful treatment for downy mildew on cucumbers and other vine crops. It is best in this case to soak the dried blossoms for a day or so in cold water. Remember, too, that if a herb is beneficial to a particular crop, a spraying of the appropriate herb will be of benefit to the plant, much as if we take added vitamins!

THE GARDEN GOURMET – RECIPES WITH HERBS
6

I could not contemplate cooking or preparing almost any food save toast (and even here herb butter may be used) without herbs. These pungent, fragrant and exciting plants offer so much natural flavour and goodness that the kitchen garden and window shelf without them are bare indeed. This chapter covers as many herbs as possible with appropriate recipes all of which are family favourites. Also included is a section featuring recipes for two.

The measurements given are for fresh herbs. If substituting dried herbs, halve the quantities.

Angelica
Angelica archangelica

The stems of this tall and luxuriantly growing herb may be candied for an after-dinner "sweetmeat". The following recipe is delicious served with cream.

Rhubarb with Angelica
500 g washed and chopped rhubarb stems (remove any tough fibres by scraping downwards)
1 tablespoon chopped angelica stalks
1 cup sugar
Water to barely cover (remember, rhubarb contains water!)

Place all in deep saucepan, cover with lid and steam slowly until fruit is tender. May be served either warm or chilled. This is also good if placed in a blender until smooth and then combined with 2 cups cream. Serve well chilled in individual glass dishes topped with a sprig of lemon balm. *Serves 8 when chilled.* The angelica counteracts the tartness of the rhubarb and may be used with other tart fruit.

Balm
Melissa officinalis

Also known as lemon balm, this "citrus" herb gives refreshing flavour to tossed salads. The following recipe is a family favourite.

Green Balm Salad
1 lettuce well washed, dried and torn into bite-sized pieces
1 tablespoon washed, dried and chopped balm leaves
2 tablespoons bean or alfalfa sprouts (either home-grown or bought)
2 tablespoons chopped chives

Judith's Dressing
3 tablespoons vegetable or olive oil
2 tablespoons white wine vinegar
¼ teaspoon salt
¼ teaspoon freshly ground black pepper
1 large clove garlic (pressed)
1 rounded teaspoon sugar
1 rounded teaspoon Dijon mustard
1 small onion very finely chopped
If using spirit vinegar used 2 rounded teaspoons sugar

Combine all ingredients in lidded jar or bottle and shake well. Pour sufficient to coat mixed salad ingredients. Toss well. *Serves 4 to 6.* Judith's Dressing is excellent for all green salads.

Lemon Balm Tea
Place 1 teaspoon washed lemon balm leaves in a cup. Fill to the brim with boiling water. Infuse for five minutes, covered. Strain off tea into second cup and sweeten with honey if desired. Never use sugar or cream in herbal teas. This is delicious when served chilled as an iced tea. *Serves 1.*

Balmed Chicken

1 medium roasting chicken
1 onion peeled and cut into quarters
1 handful washed lemon balm leaves
Salt, freshly ground pepper and flour
Vegetable oil for roasting

Wash and pat chicken dry. Stuff lemon balm and onion quarters into cavity. Sprinkle salt and pepper on bird and pat all over with flour. Place in roasting pan and drizzle oil over. Bake in moderate oven for approximately 1 hour or until done. Remove chicken from pan and using juices remaining make gravy, thickening juices with 1 tablespoon of flour or a small grated potato blended in well. Add water slowly, stirring continuously until smooth gravy is obtained. *Serves 4.*

Herbed roast potatoes would accompany this dish and provide a delicious vegetable.

Orange Balm Salad

1 thinly sliced green capsicum with seeds removed
2 large oranges
1 dessertspoon wine or cider vinegar
3 dessertspoons olive oil
1 dessertspoon finely chopped lemon balm
Salt and freshly ground pepper to taste
Extra balm leaves for garnishing

Peel oranges and, removing all pith, cut into sections. Remove any seeds. Lay in a shallow glass serving dish with green capsicum slices. Mix oil, vinegar, salt and pepper and shake well. Stir in lemon balm. Drizzle over oranges and peppers and allow to macerate for 3 to 4 hours prior to serving. This is one dish which should not be frozen or kept more than one day. It is a delicious salad with roast poultry. Garnish before serving with fresh balm leaves. *Serves 2.*

Herbed Roast Potatoes

4 medium potatoes
1 tablespoon softened butter or margarine
1 teaspoon lemon balm leaves washed and finely chopped
1 teaspoon basil leaves washed and finely chopped
Salt and freshly ground black pepper

Scrub the potatoes well and steam for 10 minutes. Remove from pan and cut each in half. Spread cut halves with a mixture of the above, wrap each potato, with cut sides together, in cooking foil and place in pan around chicken. Tear back foil to serve. *Serves 4.*

Basil
Ocimum basilicum

Frequently called the "tomato herb", it is well matched with this popular salad fruit. The dwarf form known as bush basil (*O. minimum*) may also be used in the following recipes. The purple leafed basil is better used as a garnish on creamy moulds rather than in dishes where its purple richness may add unwelcome colour contrast.

Quick Tomato Soup

1 430 g can undiluted tomato soup
1 can cream (fill soup can to measure)
1 tablespoon dry vermouth
1 teaspoon chopped basil
Extra whole basil leaves for garnishing

Combine all ingredients except whole basil leaves. Heat gently — do *not* boil. Serve into four warmed bowls and garnish with two or three basil leaves floating on top. This recipe demonstrates clearly how simple it is to use herbs to obtain extra flavour excitement — even with tinned or canned foods!

Strawberry pots planted with assorted herbs
make an attractive focal point in the garden.

Top: The robust flower heads of angelica.

Bottom: The unusual basil mint combines the flavours
of both basil and spearmint.

Mushrooms Provencale
¼ cup each tomato puree and good
    quality olive oil
½ cup chopped parsley
½ teaspoon chopped basil
1 sprig thyme (lemon, if available)
500 g fresh mushrooms (button, if
    available)
Salt and freshly ground black pepper

Place tomato puree, oil, parsley, basil and
thyme into a heavy frying pan. Cook for a
few minutes over low heat to blend well,
then add salt and pepper. Add washed
mushrooms. Simmer, stirring well, for
about two minutes. Cover pan and cook
gently for a further 5 minutes. This dish
may be served warm as a vegetable stew to
accompany roast chicken. Previously
cooked and jointed chicken may be added
for final 5 minutes of cooking to reheat.
Alternatively, if preferred, the mixture
may be placed in a bowl, covered and
cooled, then stored in the refrigerator
until required. When well chilled, it may
be served in a lettuce cup as an hors
d'oeuvre garnished with a parsley sprig for
each serving or as a salad. *Serves 6.*

Cucumber and Tomato Salad
1 large cucumber, peeled, scored with
    a fork, and sliced thinly
500 g tomatoes sliced thickly
1 tablespoon chives, finely chopped
1 tablespoon chopped basil
Salt and freshly ground pepper
1 teaspoon sugar
White wine vinegar to cover

Cover cucumber with salt and stand for
half an hour to remove excess water. Wash
well to remove salt and drain well in
colander. Combine cucumber and tomato
slices with herbs, salt, pepper and sugar in
a glass bowl and cover with vinegar. Chill
well. This dish is good with hamburgers.
Serves 4.

Tomato Sauce
500 g ripe tomatoes, or 1 425 g can
1 teaspoon chopped basil
3 tablespoons cream or yoghurt
½ teaspoon sugar
Salt and freshly ground pepper to taste

Chop tomatoes (if fresh, peel and chop)
and cook slowly in a deep uncovered pan.
No liquid is required as tomatoes produce
their own juice as they cook. Add the basil,
seasonings and sugar to the tomatoes and
simmer for approximately 20 minutes.
When smooth, turn into a blender and
puree. Just prior to serving add cream or
yoghurt.

Stuffed Basil Tomatoes
4 tomato halves
1 dessertspoon finely chopped basil
1 cup fresh breadcrumbs
½ cup shredded tasty cheddar cheese
1½ tablespoons chives, finely snipped
Freshly ground pepper
4 tablespoons, approximately, sour
    cream
Extra sour cream

Mix breadcrumbs, cheese, chives, pepper,
basil and sour cream to a firm stiff paste.
Heap mixture on tomato halves to roughly
the height of each half. Dot with a little
extra sour cream. Bake in a medium oven,
175°C, for about three-quarters of an hour
or until tomatoes are just softened. This is
a substantial hors d'oeuvre, but must be
eaten immediately it is taken from the
oven. *Serves 2.*

Bay
Laurus nobilis

Use bay with caution. Sometimes it is better to halve the suggested quantity in a recipe, particularly if introducing this herb to the family for the first time.

Beef and Bay Stew
750 g beef, cubed
2 cups beef stock
½ bunch leeks
1 small turnip
1 small carrot
6 small scrubbed potatoes
1 stick celery about 20 cm long
1 bay leaf
½ teaspoon thyme
½ lump sugar
Salt and freshly ground pepper
2 tablespoons plain flour

Roll cubed beef, with fat removed, in flour seasoned with salt and pepper. Place in casserole with stock and after bringing to the boil, simmer for three-quarters of an hour. Add the well-washed white part of the leeks thickly sliced. Peel and dice turnip and carrot and add to the dish with sliced celery and well scrubbed potatoes. Add bay leaf, thyme and sugar. Stew gently for approximately an hour and serve with thick crusty bread. *Serves 2* but this may be halved and one portion frozen.

Cauliflower with Prawns
1 large cauliflower
1 cup water
Juice 2 lemons
1 teaspoon salt
1 bay leaf
½ teaspoon thyme

Leave the cauliflower whole, but remove all outside leaves and score a cross at the stem end with a sharp knife. Wash the cauliflower. Bring water in a deep pan to the boil. Add lemon juice and salt, bay leaf and thyme and lower the vegetable into the boiling water. Once boiling again, reduce the heat and simmer for about 10 minutes or until just tender. Remove from the water and cool. Coat with the following sauce.

Prawn Sauce
1 cup shelled and deveined cooked prawns
1 tablespoon butter or margarine
1 tablespoon plain flour
1 tablespoon vermouth
1 cup milk
2 teaspoons curry powder (some palates may prefer a slightly stronger flavour, but use discretion)
Salt to taste
½ bay leaf

Melt butter and blend in flour. Stir over gentle heat until smooth. Slowly add milk, stirring all the time. Add ½ bay leaf. Continue to stir until smooth and thickened. Add curry powder and salt to taste. Stir in vermouth and allow to cool to prevent "skin" forming on sauce, cover with a piece of plastic film. When cool remove bay leaf and add prawns. Coat cauliflower with sauce and serve as an appetiser or salad. According to size of vegetable, *serves 4 to 6.*

Italian Lamb with Tomatoes

2 slices fatty bacon
1 kg lean lamb cubed (either from leg
  or shoulder and cut from the bone)
1 small onion finely chopped
1 clove garlic, finely chopped
1 cup canned egg tomatoes
½ cup dry white wine or vermouth
5 cups meat stock
1 teaspoon salt
½ teaspoon freshly ground pepper
3 tablespoons good quality olive oil
4 tablespoons plain flour
1 bay leaf
2 teaspoons basil
2 teaspoons oregano
3 egg yolks (the whites may be used
  for meringues, made in the oven
  after this dish has been cooked and
  the heat switched off)
4 tablespoons parsley, finely chopped
3 tablespoons lemon juice

Using a deep and heavy frying pan, cook
bacon in its own fat until very crisp and
brown. Discard the bacon. Add the olive oil
to the bacon fat and heat until quite hot.
Lower the heat. Place a few cubes of lamb
at a time in the hot fat mixture and toss
with spatula until golden brown on all
sides. Continue this way until all meat is
sealed and remove to a casserole. In the
same pan cook garlic and onion for five
minutes, then stir in tomatoes and wine
and bring to the boil. Simmer until the
mixture is reduced by half — approximately 10 minutes. Add the meat stock,
mixing well. Once again bring to the boil.
Sprinkle pepper, salt and flour over the
meat cubes and mix well. Pour the wine
and stock mixture over the meat and add
the bay leaf, oregano and basil. Slowly
bring to the boil over a very gentle heat,
stirring occasionally. Cover the casserole
and place it in a preheated 175°C oven for
1½ hours or until meat is tender.

Prior to serving, lift meat from dish
with a slotted spoon and keep it warm. Let
the casserole dish stand briefly and then
with a paper towel carefully lift off any fat
from the surface of the liquid. Beat the
egg yolks and add the lemon juice, mixing
well. Add a little of the gravy to the egg
yolks, then add to the warm gravy, which
should have been returned to the frying
pan. Cook gently until thickened. Do not
boil or curdling will result. Spoon sauce
over meat and sprinkle with fresh parsley.
Serve immediately accompanied by rice or
noodles. Serves 6–8.

Bergamot
Monarda didyma

Both leaves and flowers of this fragrant
plant may be used in the kitchen. The
flowers taste like honeysuckle, and when
in the country, who has not picked a
random blossom of this creeper as it
spilled over banks or fences? The flowers
are a deep wine colour and look superb
when incorporated, torn into pieces, in a
salad. They are excellent also in fruit
salad, as this recipe will show.

Bergamot Flowery Fruit Salad

3 yellow or green unpeeled apples,
  diced
1 medium bunch black grapes, seeded
2 bananas sliced and peeled
½ cubed cantaloupe (rockmelon)
Juice 2 lemons
½ cup sherry
¼ cup brandy
4 bergamot flowers, torn into pieces

Pour lemon juice over diced apples and
sliced bananas to prevent browning. Place
in glass dish. Remove seeds from grapes
by cutting almost in halves and flicking
seeds out with the point of a small knife.
Add to glass dish together with melon. Mix
wine with brandy and pour over fruit and
mix gently but well. Chill, and just before
serving toss bergamot flowers on top. This
salad may be prepared the day before
serving, but add flowers only at the last
minute. Serves 6.

Bergamot Tea (as a nightcap to induce sleep)

1 teaspoon bergamot flowers or leaves
1 cup boiling water poured over
bergamot

Infuse, covered, for five minutes. Strain. Sweeten with honey if desired. *Serves 1.*

Bergamot Sausages with Apple

750 g good quality pork sausages
1 large cooking apple, sliced thickly.
Do not peel
15 g butter or margarine, or 1
tablespoon olive oil
¾ cup stock, cider or water (stock may
be made by dissolving a bacon or
beef cube in ¾ cup hot water)
1 medium onion, sliced
1 clove garlic
1 dessertspoon finely chopped
bergamot leaves
2 tablespoons plain flour
¼ teaspoon cinnamon
Salt and freshly ground pepper to taste

Do not peel apple — there will be extra flavour — but do core! Melt butter or margarine, or heat oil, and gently saute apple until soft. Roll sausages in flour, prick and fry until golden brown. In a casserole dish place alternate layers of apple slices and sausages, together with bergamot, salt, pepper and cinnamon (lightly dusted). Pour over chosen liquid, cover tightly and simmer for an hour or until sausages are done. *Serves 2* but if only 1 portion is used, the remainder may be frozen, or will keep unfrozen in the refrigerator for 3 days.

Borage
Borago officinalis

Containing a gum-like juice which cools drinks in which a leaf or two is placed, borage is most useful in the bar as well as in the kitchen. Try a leaf in a bloody mary in lieu of celery. Add young leaves torn into small pieces to green salads. Borage leaves may be steamed and served as a vegetable. The slight hairiness of the leaves softens during cooking. Always choose young leaves. Iced cup cakes may be decorated with fresh borage flowers, but eat them the same day, as the flowers will wilt.

Red Wine Cup with Borage

1 rounded teaspoon white sugar
Thin rind of a lemon, in one piece
1 strip cucumber rind
1 bottle claret or similar red wine
Few sprigs of young borage
6–8 borage flowers (optional, but they
do look pretty!)
1 glass sherry
½ glass maraschino (optional)
½ glass brandy
A little boiling water
1 large bottle soda or mineral water

Mix rinds with half the claret. Add sugar dissolved in a little boiling water, together with borage sprigs. Stand for at least 2 hours, then pour in remaining claret, brandy, sherry and maraschino (if used). Remove borage sprigs, but float flowers and one or two tiny leaves. Add cool soda or mineral water just prior to serving. Makes approximately 12 wine-glass size servings.

Burnet
Sanguisorba minor

The Italians have a saying about pimpinella, as they call burnet, which translated is, "The salad is neither good nor fair, if Pimpinella is not there!"

This sums up the usefulness of this "cucumbery" herb. Like borage, which also has a cucumber flavour, burnet may be added to all green salads. The dainty serrated leaves also make an attractive garnish.

Mushroom Soup with Burnet
1 dessertspoon butter or margarine
1 dessertspoon plain flour
1 large cup milk
1 large cup cream
2 sprigs salad burnet, 1 sprig chervil —
* tied together*
750 g thinly sliced mushrooms
Salt, and freshly ground pepper
1 tablespoon vermouth or dry sherry
Finely chopped chives or parsley for
* garnishing*

Melt fat over low heat, blend in flour and cook very gently for 2 minutes. Gradually add the liquids, stirring well. Add herb bundle (tied to saucepan handle), mushrooms, salt and pepper, stirring constantly. Do not boil. Continue stirring and cooking until mushrooms are cooked and soup has thickened slightly. Remove bunch of herbs prior to serving and pour into 2 warmed bowls. Top with chives or parsley. *Serves 2* but if only 1 portion is required, place unused soup in a dish and cover with plastic film. This cover will prevent a "skin" forming. The soup will keep, covered, in the refrigerator for approximately 3 days.

Green Salad with Burnet
1 lettuce, medium sized
1 bunch chicory
1 head endive
About 6 burnet leaves
½ cup Judith's Dressing (see Green
* Balm Salad)*
1 dessertspoon finely chopped chives

Wash, dry and tear the lettuce and chicory into bite-sized pieces and combine with finely sliced endive in salad bowl. Chop burnet leaves which have been washed and dried and add to the bowl with the chives. Mix all well and just before serving pour dressing over salad and toss. *Serves 6–8.*

Calendula
Calendula officinalis

To use calendulas, or English marigolds as they are also known, in various dishes, gather flowers before they are hit by the sun. Wash carefully and, after removing the petals from the flower base, pat gently with paper towels. The petals may then be dried in a very low oven or placed in plastic bags and refrigerated for later use. A warning, however – on no account eat the *African* marigold! The English marigold is extremely useful as a garnish and adds dashing colour and interesting texture to cauliflower or creamed soups. Try stirring it into creamed potatoes and scrambled eggs or cream cheese dishes.

Cucumber and Marigold Soup
¼ cup marigold petals
1 cup pureed cucumber
Chopped parsley or chives
¾ cup sour cream
1 430 g can undiluted celery soup
Dash tabasco sauce

Whir all together in a blender and stir marigold petals through. Chill very well before serving in individual bowls or ramekins. Top with parsley or chives. *Serves 4.*

Camomile
Anthemis nobilis

Camomile flowers added to bath water make a therapeutic bath! They are also used to make one of the best known and appreciated herbal teas. When camomile flowers and apple mint leaves are combined they may be infused for a tea which will relieve stomach ache and vomiting. Make in the same way as camomile tea.

Camomile Tea
Infuse 1 teaspoon fresh or dried camomile flowers for 5 minutes in 1 cup boiling water. Strain and sweeten with honey if desired.

Camomile Scallop Surprise
½ cup dry white wine
½ cup fish or chicken stock
1 small onion finely chopped
2 teaspoons chopped parsley
6 sprigs camomile
1 teaspoon freshly ground pepper
¼ teaspoon salt (or to taste)
500 g scallops, sliced
1 tablespoon butter or margarine
125 g mushrooms, finely sliced
2 tomatoes, peeled and chopped
1 extra tablespoon butter or margarine
1 tablespoon flour
½ cup soft breadcrumbs

Combine wine and half stock in saucepan. Add onion, 1 teaspoon parsley, pepper and salt and 3 sprigs of camomile. Bring this mixture to the boil and add the scallops. Lower heat and gently simmer for 5 minutes. Remove from heat, strain and reserve liquid. Sauté mushrooms in 1 tablespoon butter or margarine, stirring frequently. Add tomatoes and remaining 3 camomile sprigs and cook gently for 10 minutes, stirring occasionally. Remove from heat, and discarding camomile sprigs, add scallops. In a separate pan melt the butter over a low heat and stir in flour to form a roux. Gradually add the reserved stock, stirring constantly until thickened. Combine with tomato and scallop mixture, stirring until thoroughly mixed. Divide between 2 large ramekins and sprinkle with soft breadcrumbs to form a crust and dot with a little butter or margarine. Bake in 210°C oven until golden and bubbling. Sprinkle with finely chopped parsley. This makes a hearty luncheon or supper dish and should be served with a salad and crusty bread. *Serves 2* but for 1 serving, place remainder in a covered bowl. When cool, refrigerate for no longer than 2 days. Canned salmon may be substituted for scallops.

Turkey and Rice Bake
5 tablespoons margarine or butter
4 tablespoons plain flour
½ teaspoon salt
¼ teaspoon freshly ground black pepper
5 camomile sprigs
6-8 flowers (optional — used for decorating dish before serving)
⅛ teaspoon nutmeg
600 ml milk
Extra milk (if required)
4 extra tablespoons margarine or butter
8 tablespoons each of diced onion, celery with a few leaves, and green pepper.
250 g diced mushrooms
1 sweet red pepper chopped finely
3 tablespoons dry sherry or vermouth
500 g cooked rice
¼ teaspoon freshly ground black pepper extra
¼ teaspoon extra celery salt
Paprika
500 g diced cooked turkey

Melt 5 tablespoons butter or margarine until frothy. Blend in four tablespoons flour, ½ teaspoon salt and ¼ teaspoon freshly ground black pepper. Add camomile sprigs and nutmeg and stir. Do not let brown, but cook gently for 3 minutes. Gradually add milk and stir gently as it cooks until thick and smooth. Continue to cook for another 10 minutes, stirring occasionally. Take from heat and after removing and discarding camomile sprigs, cover sauce with plastic film to prevent a "skin" from forming. Melt 4 tablespoons butter and gently sauté mushrooms, celery, onion and green pepper. Cover pan so vegetables will "sweat" slightly and steam in their own liquid for 5 minutes. Add to sauce with turkey. Cook, stirring all the time to prevent sauce from sticking, for a further 10 minutes. If too thick, add extra milk slowly. After removing from stove add red peppers and wine. Stir in well. Place rice in the bottom of a greased casserole and sprinkle with extra black pepper and celery salt. Smooth turkey mixture over rice and sprinkle with paprika. Bake in 175°C oven until heated through – 20–30 minutes. Before serving, dot with camomile flowers. *Serves 6.*

This could also be served in individual ramekins and with a green salad would make a delicious luncheon dish for cooler days. It is a splendid way to use up the leftover turkey.

Caraway
Carum carvi

Today, mainly the seed of this biennial is used in the kitchen. Caraway leaves may, however, be chopped into soups and stews as is done with parsley, and add interesting and piquant flavour. Caraway tea is an excellent drink to calm stomach cramps. Sow seed in late summer in order to have a plentiful supply of blooms the next year. Remove seed heads with care, tie brown paper bags over them to catch the seed, and hang upside-down to dry.

Caraway Tea
Pour 1 cup boiling water over 1 teaspoon seeds, lightly crushed. Stand, covered, for 5 minutes. Strain, sweeten with honey if desired. *Serves 1.*

Plain Seed Cake
½ teaspoon vanilla
1 cup plain flour
½ teaspoon baking powder
Pinch salt
½ cup margarine or butter
½ cup white sugar
3 teaspoons caraway seed
1 lightly beaten egg
Milk

Sift together flour, salt and baking powder. Rub in margarine or butter with fingertips until mixture is "crumby". Add seed and sugar and mix well. Making a well in the centre of mixture, pour in the egg and again mix well. Slowly add sufficient milk, beating all the while, to make a stiffish mix. Place in a small greased and floured loaf tin. Have oven preheated to 190°C and bake for half an hour.

Caraway Lamb Hotpot

*1½ kg stewing lamb or mutton cubed,
    with excess fat removed*
1½ tablespoons margarine or butter
*4 tablespoons flour seasoned with salt
    and freshly black ground pepper*
3 large onions peeled and sliced
8 potatoes sliced thickly
2½ cups warm meat stock
*1 dessertspoon melted margarine or
    butter*
*1 teaspoon caraway seeds in muslin
    bag*
1 slice streaky bacon, chopped

Melt margarine or butter, sauté meat and
onions together. Alternate layers of meat
and onions with sliced potatoes in a
casserole dish, finishing with a layer of
potatoes. Brush potatoes with melted
margarine or butter and top with chopped
bacon. Place bag of caraway seeds on top.
Pour over stock. Cover dish and place in a
low to medium oven for approximately 1½
hours or until meat is tender. For the last
20 minutes remove cover to allow potatoes
to turn golden and bacon to crisp. Remove
caraway seeds prior to serving. *Serves 6.*

If muslin is unavailable, take a
square of foil and, placing the seeds in the
centre, fold foil over to form a parcel,
pinching sides well. Pierce several times
with tooth pick or some similar fine
point to allow flavour to escape.

Caraway Pineapple and Grapefruit

1 large grapefruit
225 g drained pineapple pieces
1 tablespoon sherry
*2 tablespoons mild cheddar cheese,
    cubed*
1 teaspoon caraway seeds

Cut grapefruit in halves and carefully
remove fruit, reserving shells. Remove
pith from flesh and cut into dice, removing
any seeds. Combine with pineapple,
sherry and cheese in a bowl and stir in
caraway seeds. Spoon into grapefruit shell
and chill, covered, in refrigerator for 2
hours before serving as a palate cleansing
appetiser. This will keep 24 hours in the
refrigerator and would be a marvellous
"wake up" breakfast dish, as it contains
both vitamin C and protein. If serving for
breakfast, add cheese cubes just prior to
serving. *Serves 2.*

Carnation
Dianthus caryophyllus

The spicy flavour of carnation has been
used for centuries to add interest to drinks
and foods. Gather and prepare carnation
similarly to calendula. Try adding a few
petals finely chopped to your favourite
cup-cake mixture or top iced cup cakes
with the smaller carnation flowers known
as dianthus. Be sure to remove "heels" —
the green and white bases. The flowers or
petals may be used to garnish summer-
time salads and desserts and add a talking
point when floated in fruit cup or punch.
The following cordial is a very tasty drop!

Carnation Cordial

*500 g fresh, washed carnation petals
    (red for preference — they seem to
    have more flavour)*
Small bottle of good brandy
½ cup water
250 g white sugar
1 whole clove
½ stick cinnamon

Carefully examine the flower petals,
removing all stems and sepals. Place in a
glass or earthenware container with a lid.
Do not use metal, as the spirit will corrode
it. Add the spices. Pour brandy into the
container and seal firmly. Store in a cool
dark place for 6 weeks without removing
the cover. At the end of this period, mix
sugar and water and boil for 15 minutes to
make a syrup. Strain brandy mixture and
stir the syrup into the brandy. Bottle and
seal. This makes a pleasant liqueur or
cordial to have with after-dinner coffee.

Chervil

Anthriscus cerefolium

Chervil is one herb that is happiest when grown in part shade. Its delicate soft green foliage resembles a very soft, lacy parsley. It is light in flavour and has many uses. It adds piquancy to soups, sauces and salads and as it enhances other flavours, chervil is often included in custards and liqueurs of various kinds. The following sauce is excellent to serve with fish or chicken.

Chervil Sauce

½ cup chicken stock
½ cup milk
Salt and pepper to taste
1 small onion, finely chopped
1 tablespoon butter or margarine
1½ tablespoons yoghurt or commercial sour cream
2 tablespoons plain flour
2 tablespoons chervil, parsley and chives mixed
1 teaspoon lemon juice

Sauté the onion in melted butter or margarine. Mix in flour until smooth. Do not let it brown. Add stock and milk combined and, stirring, simmer until smooth. Strain to remove onion pieces and stir in the herbs and lemon juice. Just prior to serving add the yoghurt or sour cream.

Chervil Soup

750 ml chicken or vegetable hot stock
Salt and pepper to taste
3 tablespoons butter or margarine
1 raw potato grated
½ cup cold water
1 tablespoon cream
3 tablespoons chervil

Melt butter or margarine over gentle heat and stir in the potato. Cook gently until slightly softened. Be careful not to let it brown. Add chervil and sauté gently. Stir in cold water and continue cooking very gently, for 3–4 minutes. Add hot stock and salt and pepper to taste. Cook for a further 20 minutes. Add cream just prior to serving. *Serves 4–5.*

Spinach Soup with Chervil

850 ml beef stock
2 cups pureed spinach
1 dessertspoon sour cream
1 tablespoon sherry
1 tablespoon chervil, finely chopped
Salt and freshly ground pepper

Cook pureed spinach (may be prepared in a blender) gently in beef stock for about 10 minutes. Add sherry, adjust seasoning with salt and pepper to taste. Pour into warmed bowls and top each serving with a dollop of sour cream and chopped chervil. Any remaining soup may be frozen for later, but in this case do not add cream and chervil. These can be added when the soup is finally served. *Serves 2–3.*

Chives
Allium schoenoprasum

This herb may be used in any dish other than sweet ones or beverages. Chives tempt the appetite of invalids, so when preparing meals for the sick room it would be advisable to flavour or garnish them with chives. Curiously, small quantities of finely chopped leaves, mixed with their mash, are reputed to be beneficial for newly hatched turkeys and chickens!

Chives are not only useful as a flavouring herb, but add attractive garnish as well when sprinkled on top of soups, hors d'oeuvres or salads. The following sauce requires no cooking and makes a tasty addition to boiled meats.

Seven Herb Sauce
3 hard-boiled eggs
½ lemon
Salt and pepper to taste
1 tablespoon salad oil
2 tablespoons chopped chives
1 tablespoon chopped mixed herbs,
  including dill, chervil, tarragon,
  parsley, salad burnet and savory
1 cup sour cream thinned with a little
  milk

Separate carefully the yolks from the whites of the eggs. Mash the yolks well with a fork. Add the oil and mix to a smooth paste. Add salt and pepper and juice of the half lemon. Add herbs to mixture and mix well. Stir in cream; add chopped egg whites and mix well.

Chived French Omelette
6 eggs
1 tablespoon butter or margarine
1 tablespoon snipped chives
1½ tablespoons cold water
Salt
Freshly ground pepper
½ teaspoon marjoram

Break eggs into a basin and beat well with a fork and when well mixed add water, seasonings and herbs. Melt butter or margarine in a pan until it sizzles. Tilt the pan so the base is thoroughly covered with fat. Pour in egg mixture. With a broad knife or spatula quickly lift up the sides of the omelette all round the pan to allow the mixture to run underneath. Do this a few times and then cut it once across the centre. The bottom of the omelette will be firm and golden, while the top remains creamy and not quite set. Lift the omelette with an egg slice, fold it over, halve it and serve immediately on two hot plates. *Serves 2.*

Chived Potatoes
500 g peeled potatoes (canned may also
  be used)
1 dessertspoon snipped chives
2 tablespoons butter or margarine
Freshly ground pepper

Boil potatoes and cut into dice. If using canned variety, drain well and cut into dice. Melt butter or margarine and toss in potato cubes. Sauté until golden, shaking pan often. Add chives and pepper to pan and shake pan to coat cubes with chives. Serve immediately.

Coriander
Coriandrum sativum

The lacy foliage of coriander is rather bitter, but the seeds when crushed give delightful flavour to gingerbread, pies and breads. They can also be included in poultry stuffing and sausages. The crushed seeds also have a sweet perfume and are frequently added to potpourri to enhance dried flowers.

Coriander Veal Chops
2 large veal chops
2 tablespoons dried breadcrumbs
1 clove garlic
1 teaspoon crushed coriander
1 tablespoon plain flour
1 beaten egg
4 tablespoons oil
Grated rind 1 lemon
Salt and freshly ground pepper

Crush garlic and coriander together. It is easier if coriander seeds have already been crushed lightly. Mix with breadcrumbs, salt and pepper. Heat oil in pan and add lemon rind. Roll chops in flour and then dip in beaten egg and finally seasoned crumbs. Place chops in heated oil and cook in 190°C oven until brown and crisp. These are also delicious cold with salad. *Serves 2.*

Arabian Stuffed Peppers
12 medium sized green capsicums
500 g minced steak
2 cups cooked rice
2 cups chicken or vegetable stock
2 tablespoons pine nuts
2 onions finely chopped
½ teaspoon cinnamon, ground
1 tablespoon chopped black olives
2 teaspoons crushed coriander seed
2 peeled and diced tomatoes
Salt and pepper

Mix meat, rice, pine nuts, onions, coriander, cinnamon, olives, tomatoes, salt and pepper; remove a slice from the top of each capsicum and remove seeds. Fill with meat mixture. Replace tops and put in shallow baking dish. Pour stock over and bake in 175°C oven for an hour, basting frequently. Any remaining meat mixture may be formed into small balls and placed in dish with stuffed capsicums. *Serves 6.*

Use wet hands when handling minced steak and the meat will not stick to the fingers.

Coriander Water
This delightful recipe is taken from *A Perfect School of Instruction for the Officers of the Month* (1682) by Giles Rose, one of the Master Cooks to Charles II.

"Take a handful of coriander seeds, break them and put them into about a quart [1 litre] of water, and so let it stand, put in a quarter of a pound [113 g] of sugar, and when your sugar is melted and the water well taken with the taste of the seeds, then strain it out through a cloath and drink it at your pleasure . . ."

Dandelion
Taraxacum officinale

Probably one of the most maligned herbs because of its habit of popping up almost anywhere, dandelion is nevertheless very useful and beneficial.

Dandelion Wine
2 litres dandelion flowers in bud
3 lemons
1 g yeast
8 litres water
½ piece toast
2 kg white sugar

Boil flowers in water for 20 minutes. Strain the boiling liquid on to the sugar. Halve lemons, peel them (reserving rind) and remove the seeds. Put the fruit into the mixture. Place yeast on the toast and float it on the partially cooled mixture. It will take about 2 days to ferment. Remove lemon pieces, toast and yeast. Add the rind, and bottle in sterilised containers. Keep for approximately 3 weeks before drinking.

Dandelion Salad
¼ cup unopened dandelion buds
250 ml very young and tender
  dandelion leaves
2 rashers bacon
1 tablespoon Judith's Dressing (see
  Green Balm Salad)

Wash leaves and flower buds and dry thoroughly between paper towels. Fry bacon until crisp in its own fat in a pan. Remove bacon and reserve fat. Sauté buds in fat until they burst. Crumble bacon when cool into a salad bowl and add buds and torn leaves. Pour over dressing, toss and serve immediately. *Serves 2.*

Dill
Anethum graveolens

This feathery foliaged herb with its slight tinge of blue grows and is used throughout Europe, particularly by the Nordic countries, where it is as popular as is parsley in other countries. Both foliage and seeds are used and if either is added to the cooking pot containing cabbage it takes away that "tell-tale" odour and the vegetable itself is rendered more digestible. I never serve coleslaw unless I've included a teaspoon of seed or a tablespoon of foliage. Cucumber, too, benefits from this herb — think of *dill* pickles, favourites for many years. Fish or cheese dishes are enhanced by dill.

Dill Pickles
Select or, if home-grown, pick cucumbers 6–8 cm (at most) long and place in the coolest section of the refrigerator — *not* freezer — 24 hours prior to using. Twelve are needed for this recipe.
4 × 8 cm sprays of dill
2 grape leaves
1 sprig tarragon
1 spray basil
1 sage leaf
1 small spike rosemary
4 cloves garlic
1 dry chilli
½ bay leaf
6 crushed peppercorns
⅛ teaspoon caraway seeds
¾ cup salt

Place all ingredients listed for brine in a large saucepan. Add the crisp cucumbers and cover with boiling water. Place lid on the saucepan and stand until contents are cool. When cold, place pickles in a large screw-top jar, ensuring the brine fully covers the cucumbers. Store for 3 weeks before using. On opening the jar a little mildew may be noticed on the surface of the brine. Merely remove this and enjoy your pickles! After opening, store the jar in the refrigerator.

Dill Potatoes

250 g cooked potatoes cut into thick slices
1 tablespoon butter or margarine, or oil
1 small onion finely chopped
¼ teaspoon garlic juice
¼ cup chicken or vegetable stock
1 tablespoon plain flour
Salt and freshly ground pepper
2 tablespoons sour cream or milk
½ tablespoon finely chopped dill

Melt butter or margarine, or heat oil and sauté the onion gently until transparent. Add flour and sauté once more, being careful not to burn the flour. Blend in stock, stirring until smooth. Add salt, garlic juice and potatoes, bringing to the boil. Add dill and simmer for 3 minutes. Add cream or milk and reheat. This is an excellent accompaniment for fish dishes and any potatoes remaining may be stored, covered, in refrigerator for up to 3 days and reheated. *Serves 2.*

Cheesy-Dill Spread

⅛ kg cream cheese
2 teaspoons dill seed
Chopped dill foliage
2 teaspoons cream
2 tablespoons chopped chives
2 teaspoons lemon juice
Salt and freshly ground pepper to taste

Beat or blend cream and cheese together, add the rest of the ingredients except dill foliage, and mix well. Spread on crisp crackers and garnish with a sprinkling of dill foliage on each. This also makes a tasty spread for sandwiches. A little sliced celery added to the sandwiches provides texture contrast and delicious flavour.

Elder
Sambucus nigra

The elder or elderberry grows to approximately 2 metres in height and is very showy. In rural areas, the berries were often brewed into wine and both leaves and flowers may be brewed into tea. An old musical instrument called the sambuca, which had a tone similar to a trombone, was fashioned from elder wood and gave the plant its generic name, while *nigra* refers to the juicy black berries that form heavy clusters in late summer.

Elder Wine

" To every gallon [4½ litres] of water a peck [500 g] of berries. To every gallon [4½ litres] of juice three pounds [1½ kg] of sugar, half [250 g] of ground ginger, six cloves and one pound [500 g] of raisins. A quarter of a pint [150 ml] of brandy to every gallon [4½ litres] of wine and three or four tablespoons of brewer's yeast to every nine gallons [40 litres] of water. Pour boiling water on the berries and let them stand covered for 24 hours. Then strain the whole through a bag or sieve, breaking the berries to extract the juice. Measure the liquid, and to every gallon [4½ litres] allow three pounds [1½ kg] of sugar. Boil the juice with the sugar and other ingredients for one hour, skimming the whole time. Let it ferment for a fortnight, add the brandy. Bung up the cask, and let the wine remain thus six months before bottling." (*Travels Around Our Village* by E. G. Hayden)

Some recipes stipulate that the berries should be gathered at midday on a warm, sunny day, when they are at their juiciest.

Elderberry Dumplings

Sauce
1 cup washed elderberries, stems
   removed
½ cup sugar
½ tablespoon flour
1 tablespoon lemon juice
½ cup water

Dumplings
½ cup plain flour
¾ teaspoon baking powder
Pinch salt
¼ teaspoon grated lemon rind
⅛ cup milk
1 slightly beaten egg
⅛ teaspoon coriander

For the sauce, place elderberries in a saucepan. In a bowl mix sugar and flour and blend with water and lemon juice. Pour mixture over the berries and slowly bring to the boil, stirring often to prevent sticking. Keep berries warm over *very* low heat. To make the dumplings, sift flour together with baking powder, coriander and salt. Add the sugar and grated lemon rind. Combine egg and milk and, pouring onto the dry ingredients, stir until well blended. Pour the elderberry mixture into a fireproof dish and drop four spoonsful of dumpling mixture onto the sauce. Bake in a hot oven, 190°C, for 25 minutes or until the tops of the dumplings are golden. Serve warm with whipped cream. *Serves 2, 2 per serve.*

Blackberries or blueberries may be substituted for the elderberries if preferred or more easily obtained.

Elder Blossom and Peppermint Tea
1 litre boiling water
1 handful elder blossom
1 handful peppermint

Pour water over blossom and mint and infuse for 5 minutes before straining. Sweeten with honey if wished, though the blossoms themselves will add a sweetness to the brew. *Serves 6.*

Fennel
Foeniculum vulgare

The seeds, bulbous stem and base and foliage of fennel are all useful. Fennel sauce is particularly good with fish. The flavour is similar to that of aniseed. The leaves, which are feathery, give interesting flavour when finely chopped into salads, while the stem may also be served in salads or steamed and served in a white sauce as a vegetable.

Fennel Sauce
2 tablespoons finely chopped fennel
Salt and freshly ground black pepper to
   taste
1 cup cream
1 teaspoon honey
1 tablespoon lemon juice

Whip cream until thickened. Blend in lemon juice and honey. Lastly add fennel, salt and pepper. Serve with steamed or baked fish.

Fennel Sausage

1 cup dried breadcrumbs
500 g lean minced beef
1 egg beaten well
1 tablespoon fennel seeds
1 clove garlic
1 finely chopped onion
Salt and finely ground pepper
1 large floured cloth

Place beef, seeds, garlic, onion, salt and pepper in a bowl. Add beaten egg and mix well together. Spread the floured cloth on table or bench top. Form meat mixture into a sausage with wet hands and place in the centre of the floured cloth and roll the cloth round well, tying at each end with white string. Place in a large pan of boiling water, cover and boil approximately 2 hours. Lift out very carefully and place on a plate. Unfold the cloth and roll the sausage in breadcrumbs and leave to cool. This serves 4, is delicious and will keep for a week, providing cold cuts for sandwiches, salads, etc.

Fennel and Potato Cake

500 g potatoes peeled and sliced thinly
3 teaspoons fennel seed
2 tablespoons butter or margarine
Salt and freshly ground pepper
1 small jar cream

Grease a baking dish with butter or margarine and place a layer of potatoes in the bottom. Sprinkle with one teaspoon fennel seeds, salt and pepper and dot with butter or margarine. Repeat layers and pour cream over the top. Bake in 175°C oven for approximately one hour. If the potatoes become too crisp, cover with foil. Test with a fork — when soft in the centre the cake is ready. Serve hot. *Serves 4.*

Garlic
Allium sativum

Only the bulb of this herb is used. It is formed of separate bulblets or "cloves" covered with a thin, papery skin which is removed prior to using. Garlic may be crushed or chopped finely for various dishes and sometimes the juice only is required. This may be obtained with a garlic press or by pushing the back of one spoon against another holding a clove. The resulting juice is then strained off. If a dish containing garlic is cooked slowly for a long time the flavour imparted is delicious but inoffensive to those who object to garlic and its smell. A good trick worth remembering when garlic is on the breath is to chew some Italian or smooth-leaf parsley, which is a breath freshener. The following soup recipe calls for the dish to be served icy cold. If necessary, float an ice-cube in it. It is virtually a liquid salad, a simple version of the famous Spanish gazpacho, and is best made in a blender or food processor. Garlic is also an excellent flavour additive to hot soups and stews.

Gazpacho

500 g tomatoes, fresh or canned
850 ml tomato juice
1 clove garlic finely chopped
1 green pepper, seeded and cut into dice
1 cucumber, peeled and cut into dice
1 large onion, chopped
2 teaspoons rosemary
2 teaspoons basil
Freshly ground black pepper
Salt
1 tablespoon salad oil
2 tablespoons white vinegar or lemon juice
Tabasco sauce to taste

Blend all ingredients. It may be necessary to do this in small quantities, e.g. pepper and half juice and then cucumber and remaining juice with herbs, onion and half tomatoes, remaining tomatoes with oil and vinegar. Mix well and add salt, pepper and tabasco to taste. *Chill well* and serve with toasted sippets or croutons. *Serves 4–5.*

This is a very filling dish, but at the same time very low in calories!

Stuffed Steak Rolls

2 slices stewing steak pounded thin and fat removed
¼ cup red wine
¼ cup stock or water
2 tablespoons soft breadcrumbs
1 rasher bacon with rind removed
1 teaspoon each chopped parsley and celery
1 tablespoon oil
1 small onion finely chopped
1 dessertspoon melted butter or margarine
1 tablespoon plain flour
1 clove garlic, finely chopped
Salt and freshly ground pepper

Cut steak into strips after pounding to half its thickness. Combine breadcrumbs, diced bacon, celery, onion, herbs and melted butter. Season with salt and pepper. Spread stuffing on steak strips and roll up, securing each with a toothpick. Roll in flour and fry in oil until juices are sealed and rolls are lightly browned. Place in a heatproof dish, add liquids, cover and simmer in a moderate oven (175°C) for approximately 2 hours. Remove toothpicks prior to serving with rice, noodles or creamed potatoes and a salad. *Serves 2* but if serving only 1, the remainder, with gravy, may be frozen.

Left: Fennel's aniseed-flavoured base is used
in salads and sauces.

Right: Apple geranium, one of the many
fragrant-leaved geraniums.

Top: Heartsease, a member of the violet family, is today
used principally for decoration.
Bottom: The large, scented leaves of peppermint geranium.

Geranium

Pelargonium sp.

The scented-leaf geraniums add infinite pleasure to the garden and are also a delight when incorporated into flower arrangements, adding their particular fragrance to the room. I am frequently asked if they possess any culinary value. The answer is a definite "Yes!" Try flavouring milk puddings or custards with washed rose, lemon or apple geranium leaves. Rose geranium leaves also add subtle flavour and fragrance if placed in the base of cake tins when plain batter is poured over them. When the cake is turned out, the leaves peel off. The following pudding may be eaten hot or cold, served with cream.

Rice and Geranium Pudding

2 scant tablespoons rice (raw)
1 tablespoon treacle
850 ml milk
1 dessertspoon butter or margarine
3 lemon or coconut geranium leaves

Mix rice and treacle in an ovenproof dish. Gradually blend in the milk, mixing well. Dot the top of the pudding with butter or margarine and lay washed geranium leaves on top. Bake in 135°C oven for about one and a half hours. *Serves 4.*

Baked Porcupine Apples with Geranium Leaves

2 green cooking apples
1 tablespoon apple or red currant jelly
1 egg white
1 dessertspoon sugar
1 dessertspoon toasted almond slivers
2 rose geranium leaves
1 teaspoon butter

Wash apples, core them and cut slits around the top of the apple — this prevents splitting during cooking. Place half a teaspoon of butter or margarine in each apple and fill hollow of each with jelly and top with a rose geranium leaf. Stand the apples in a little water in a heat proof dish and bake in a medium oven until just soft. In the meantime, whip egg white with sugar to form a meringue. Remove apples from the oven and cover with meringue. Spike with almond slivers and return to a slow oven for 10 minutes or until meringue is lightly browned. The rose geranium leaves would have crisped while apples were cooking and are perfectly edible. *Serves 2.*

Horehound
Marrubium vulgare

The generic or botanical name of this herb — *Marrubium* — is from the Hebrew *marrob* meaning a bitter juice, and this describes the flavour well! The grey, somewhat velvety leaves are heavily veined and this herb, like chervil and bergamot, does best in light shade. Horehound candy was popular in years gone by for soothing coughs.

Candied Honey
"Boil some horehound until the juice is extracted. Boil up some sugar to a feather height, add your juice to the sugar, and let it boil till it is again the same height. Stir it until it begins to grow thick, then pour it on to a dish with sugar and when fairly cool cut into squares. Excellent sweetmeat for colds and coughs." (*The Family Herbal* 1810 by R. Thornton)

Horseradish
Cochlearia amoracia

It is, of course, the tapering root which is used to make horseradish sauce. It takes two years for the root to develop and in the meantime the young leaves of horseradish are pleasant in salads. As well as being the traditional roast beef accompaniment, horseradish may also be used in dips, seafood savouries or shrimp cocktails. To make horseradish sauce more easily use a blender to grate the herb, otherwise it is a slow and laborious process.

Apple and Horseradish Salad
1 large red-skinned eating apple
½ teaspoon horseradish relish
1 tablespoon sour cream
Juice 1 lemon
2 lettuce cups
Parsley, mint or watercress

Grate apple — leave skin on for extra colour. Mix with lemon juice and horseradish relish. Spoon into lettuce cups and garnish with sprigs of the chosen herb. Serve immediately. This makes a delicious appetiser and *serves 2.*

Horseradish and Apple Sauce (to accompany fish)
6 large apples, peeled and grated
1 glass lemon juice (this prevents the apple from turning brown)
2 tablespoons sugar
2 tablespoons grated horseradish
1 glass dry white wine
Salt to taste
Add the sugar, juice and wine to the grated apple. Mix in the horseradish (more may be added if taste dictates). Keep stirring until the sauce appears to froth a little.

Shellfish Dip

1 cup prepared mayonnaise
½ cup cottage cheese
1 medium onion, peeled and finely
    chopped
3 tablespoons freshly grated
    horseradish
Salt and freshly ground pepper
⅛ teaspoon paprika
½ apple, peeled and grated
1 teaspoon lemon juice
1 tablespoon butter or margarine
1 tablespoon soft breadcrumbs
1 tablespoon chopped parsley
¼ teaspoon marjoram
¼ teaspoon basil
¼ teaspoon thyme
2 tablespoons chervil
½ teaspoon rosemary
½ teaspoon winter savory
1 teaspoon tarragon

Melt butter or margarine and sauté onion and horseradish. Add breadcrumbs and fry until golden. Remove from heat and cool. Add seasonings, mixed herbs, apple and lemon juice. Mix very well with cheese and mayonnaise. Chill prior to serving.

Hyssop
Hyssopus officinalis

Hyssop flowers and tops are used in making some continental sausages as the herb helps to counteract the fat contained in the meat. It also may be cooked with fat fish such as eel, and adds piquancy to fruit pies such as apricot or peach. Just ¼ teaspoon of the finely chopped leaves sprinkled over the fruit before the top crust is added is sufficient.

Hyssop Tea

1 teaspoon hyssop leaves
1 cup boiling water
Honey, if sweetening is required

Pour boiling water over leaves, stand for 5 minutes and strain. Sweeten with honey if desired. *Serves 1.*

Only glass or china pots or receptacles should be used for brewing herb teas as the flavour is much better than when made in a metal teapot.

Apricot Delight

12 apricot halves (fresh or canned)
2 egg whites
Pinch salt
¼ teaspoon hyssop
8 hyssop flowers for garnishing
½ cup whipped cream
1 tablespoon sugar (if using fresh
    apricots)

Whizz apricots (and sugar if used) in the blender with hyssop to puree them. Whip egg whites with salt and then fold through the pureed apricots. Spoon into 4 serving dishes and chill well. Top with whipped cream and before serving garnish each with two hyssop flowers. *Serves 4.*

Juniper
Juniperus communis

This is a most aromatic plant as the needle-like leaves are full of resinous oil. The berries may be dried in a shaded but warm place. It is, however, important to use them within 12 months as they lose their aroma and valued properties if kept longer. The berries are used in many ways. It has been found that, when burnt, a gas is released from the berries which has a germ-killing quality and is also a disinfectant — an excellent way to purify the air in an invalid's room! Juniper berries are also used to enhance the flavour of chicken dishes and various stews and casseroles. They are particularly good when incorporated in marinades for game.

Chicken with Juniper
1½ kg chicken
¼ cup soft breadcrumbs
12 crushed juniper berries
½ teaspoon each of marjoram, thyme, basil and tarragon, or 2 teaspoons mixed herbs
1 peeled and finely chopped onion
1 teaspoon grated lemon rind
1 cup dry white wine
2 pieces celery about 15 cm long, cut into slices
2 medium carrots, peeled and sliced thinly
3 shallots chopped into small pieces
1 tablespoon butter or margarine
Salt and freshly ground pepper

Stuff the chicken with seasoning made by combining breadcrumbs, berries, lemon rind, salt and pepper. Truss the bird and smear with the butter or margarine and place it in a roasting pan. Add vegetables and pour wine over the chicken. Cover the pan with foil, tucking it over the edges. Bake in a moderate oven — 175°C — for approximately 1½ hours. It may be necessary to lower the heat. Lift the chicken on to a warmed serving dish and pour wine and vegetables over it. Potatoes baked in their jackets would be a good accompaniment. Serve with sour cream and chives. *Serves 4.*

Cheesy Veal with Juniper Berries
2 thick veal fillets
1 small onion finely chopped
½ teaspoon garlic juice
1 dessertspoon butter or margarine
4 slices gruyère cheese
¼ cup fresh breadcrumbs
Salt and freshly ground pepper
4 crushed juniper berries
1 extra teaspoon butter or margarine

Sauté onion in butter or margarine until transparent. Add the salt, pepper, garlic juice and berries. Tip mixture into a casserole. Place fillets, with any fat removed, on top of the onion, then top the fillets with cheese slices. Sprinkle thickly with breadcrumbs to form a crust and dot with extra teaspoon of butter or margarine. Bake, uncovered in a moderate oven (175°C) for 45 minutes. *Serves 2.*

Juniper Butter Sauce
4 tablespoons melted butter or margarine
1 teaspoon finely chopped garlic
1 large onion peeled and finely chopped
4 lightly crushed juniper berries
3 teaspoons lemon juice
Salt and freshly ground pepper
1 tablespoon chopped parsley

Sauté onion and garlic gently in the butter or margarine. Add the berries, lemon juice, seasonings and parsley. This yields about 6 tablespoons and is delicious served with baked potatoes, asparagus or as a fondue sauce for meat or chicken. It is necessary to crush the juniper berries lightly to release the flavour.

Lavender
Lavendula sp.

The foliage of all lavenders is silvery grey and fragrant. The plants should be grown in well-drained soil and do not care for wet winter "feet". Leaves that are to be used in the kitchen — yes, this joy of perfumes *can* be used to flavour food! — should be about 8 cm long. Wash them thoroughly and pat with paper towels, very gently, to dry. The flowers should also be washed and similarly dried. A spray of lavender foliage may be placed in the pan when roasting a chicken.

Garlic Prawn and Ham Soup
60 g fresh green or frozen peas
1 small onion chopped finely
1½ tablespoons olive oil
½ teaspoon finely chopped garlic
60 g finely diced ham
90 g raw rice
125 g prawns (cooked, shelled and
*   deveined)*
Salt and freshly ground pepper
2 tablespoons finely chopped blanched
*   almonds*
850 ml of lavender beef stock, made by
*   infusing 8 heads of lavender in hot*
*   stock and then straining.*

Sauté onion and garlic gently in hot oil. Add ham and sauté this also. Bring stock to the boil and add rice, cooking briskly for 12 minutes. Add peas, salt and pepper. Cook for 10 minutes and add onion mixture and prawns. Heat gently, so as not to toughen prawns. This *serves 2* as a generous main meal.

Lavender Tea
1 teaspoon leaves or flowers
1 cup boiling water
Honey to sweeten

Pour water over foliage or flowers and infuse for 5 minutes. Strain and sweeten with honey. *Serves 1.*

Lavender Pineapple Appetiser
1 850 g can pineapple pieces with
*   juices drained off, or 1 fresh*
*   pineapple, peeled, cored and diced*
1 dessertspoon finely chopped lavender
*   leaves*
½ cup brandy
Lavender flowers to garnish
1 tablespoon sugar if using fresh
*   pineapple*

If using fresh pineapple, sprinkle the diced fruit with the sugar. Toss in the lavender leaves and mix well. Pour brandy over and chill well. Divide between 6 small serving dishes and garnish each with a lavender flower before serving. This delicious "opener" cleanses the palate before the main course and may be prepared 24 hours ahead.

Lavender and Spice Oranges
150 ml water
1 cup red wine such as claret
6 tablespoons sugar
4 cloves
6 slices lemon
12 lavender leaves
1 x 8 cm piece of cinnamon
6 segmented oranges

Combine water, wine, sugar, spices, lemon and lavender. Bring to the boil and then simmer over reduced heat. Stir occasionally and when syrupy remove from heat and cool. Place segmented oranges in a glass serving dish and pour the strained syrup over. Chill for at least 4 hours. May be served with whipped cream. *Serves 8.*

Lemon Verbena
Aloysia citriodora

The leaves and occasionally the flower of this shrub, native to South America and introduced into Great Britain in 1761, are used to impart sharp lemony fragrance to potpourris and sachets. The merest brushing releases the clear fresh fragrance. A tea made from the leaves is frequently drunk in Spain. An excellent substitute for lemon rind, the fresh or dried leaves add a tang to fish dishes, jellies or trifles, whilst the fresh leaves add zest to salads and fish-based sandwiches. Both in the garden and in the house, the foliage aids in repelling flying insects.

Lemon Verbena Tossed Salad
*2 tablespoons Judith's Dressing
(see Green Balm Salad)
1 lettuce well-washed, dried and torn
into pieces
1 dessertspoon finely chopped fresh
lemon verbena leaves
2 finely sliced eschallots or one finely
sliced spring onion
¼ cup finely sliced button mushrooms*

Combine last four ingredients, mix well and chill. Just prior to serving pour Judith's Dressing over and toss well.

Lemon Verbena Tea
*1 dessertspoon fresh lemon verbena
leaves or
1 teaspoon dried lemon verbena leaves*

Pour 1 cup boiling water over leaves and infuse for 5 minutes. Strain. If desired, sweeten with a half a teaspoon of honey.

Lovage
Levisticum officinale

This herb has a most unusual yeast-like flavour and has been looked on in many countries as an aphrodisiac! It is also considered to be a natural deodorant in some areas of Europe. Lovage tea stimulates the digestive organs and is a diuretic, and lovage leaves placed on wounds have proved an effective antibiotic and antiseptic. It would be worthwhile to include it in the bath to take advantage of its deodorant qualities. The appearance of the herb is similar to that of celery and indeed can replace celery in dishes when that vegetable is unobtainable. It is widely used in soups, casseroles and stews. Until familiar with it, it is wise to use lovage with discretion.

Lovage and Ham Spread
*250 g minced cooked ham
2 tablespoons lovage leaves, very
finely chopped, or 2 tablespoons
lovage seeds
190 g butter or margarine
¼ teaspoon paprika*

Mix ham, lovage and butter or margarine together (a blender or food processor would be ideal for this). Stir in the paprika and mix well. Spread on crisp crackers garnished with parsley or use as a sandwich spread. This quantity yields about ¾ cup.

Lovage Tea
This is more like a broth than most other herb teas, so season with a little herb salt and enjoy it as an appetising calorie-free snack.

*1 teaspoon lovage leaves, chopped
1 cup boiling water
Celery or herb salt*

Pour water over leaves and steep for 5 minutes. Strain if desired and season with salt. *Serves 1.*

Lovage Soup

1 tablespoon flour
1 tablespoon chopped lovage
1 tablespoon parsley (for garnishing)
1 tablespoon chives
1 tablespoon butter or margarine
1½ cups stock (beef or vegetable)
1 tablespoon cream

Sauté flour in butter or margarine. Add stock and cook for 20 minutes. Place lovage and chives into a large bowl. Add hot stock and stir very well. Stand for half an hour and reheat. Remove from heat, add cream and serve immediately with parsley sprinkled on top. Any remaining soup will keep, covered, in refrigerator for 3 days. *Serves 2–3.*

Lovage Cordial

1 tablespoon freshly gathered lovage
   seeds
850 ml good quality brandy
4 tablespoons white sugar

Crush the seeds lightly in a mortar with a pestle or if tied in a clean cloth they may be crushed with a wooden rolling pin. Add the seeds to the brandy with the sugar and stir well. Place in a sterilised container and cork. Stand in a cool dark place for 2 months, occasionally shaking the container. Pour the cordial through a filter. Rebottle and cork and serve at room temperature. This yields about 850 ml.

Marjoram
Origanum majorana

The velvety leaves of this pungent herb combine well with many different foods but as the flavour is very strong it is advisable to use marjoram with discretion. It is very suitable to be included in the bouquet garni so favoured for soups and stews. This consists of a bay leaf, a sprig of thyme and, of course, marjoram or its stronger brother, oregano. Marjoram adds interesting flavour to egg and potato dishes as well as to mushrooms. It enhances liver pâté or sausages and is traditionally used in the Polish sausage, kielbasa.

Lamb Chops with Herb Sauce

1 teaspoon chopped marjoram
1 clove garlic, crushed (optional)
1 teaspoon basil
1 teaspoon finely chopped parsley
½ teaspoon salt
½ teaspoon freshly ground pepper
4 large lamb chops
½ cup dry white wine such as chablis
   or white burgundy
½ cup butter or margarine
1 teaspoon cornflour

In a small bowl combine marjoram, basil, salt and pepper and garlic (if used) and press the mixture into both sides of the chops. Melt the butter in a frying pan and lightly fry the chops on both sides for about 3 minutes. Add a quarter of a cup of white wine and simmer gently over low heat for approximately 20 minutes with pan tightly covered. Mix cornflour smoothly in remaining wine and when cooking time is completed for the chops, place them on a warm serving dish and keep hot. Add the wine and cornflour to the pan. Increase the heat and stir smoothly to prevent lumping and to mix the juices from the chops. When sauce is thick, stir in the chopped parsley. Pour sauce over chops or pass separately in a gravy boat. *Serves 4.*

Mushrooms Provençale

*500 g fresh mushrooms or the
  equivalent of drained canned button
  mushrooms
¼ cup olive oil
¼ cup tomato puree
2 sprigs marjoram
½ cup chopped parsley
1 bay leaf
Salt and freshly ground pepper*

Warm olive oil in a heavy frying pan. Add
the herbs and tomato puree. Add washed
and sliced fresh mushrooms or drained
canned ones. Stir and simmer over gentle
heat for 2 minutes. Add salt and pepper
then, covering the pan, cook mixture very
gently for 2 minutes. Remove bay leaf.
Excellent as a warm sauce to accompany
barbecued meats or may be served well
chilled as a salad. *Serves 4* as a salad.

Marjoram Potato Cakes

*2 medium boiled potatoes
1 tablespoon butter
Salt and freshly ground pepper
1 egg (beaten)
1 teaspoon chopped marjoram
½ teaspoon chopped parsley*

Mash potatoes while still warm until
smooth. Mix butter or margarine, salt and
pepper into potatoes and add marjoram
and parsley. When cool, add the well
beaten egg. With floured hands shape into
flat cakes and fry in butter. These are
delicious for breakfast when served with
bacon.

Herbed Bachelor Toast

*½ clove minced or crushed garlic
¼ teaspoon chopped marjoram
¼ teaspoon snipped chives
1 tablespoon butter or margarine
2 thick slices French bread
2 tablespoons grated tasty cheese*

Mix garlic and butter together. Blend in
marjoram and chives. Spread mixture on
the French bread slices and top lavishly
with the grated cheese. Place in a 190°C
oven until the bread is golden and the
cheese has melted into the butter or
margarine. Serve at once. This makes an
interesting meal "starter" or a substantial
snack.

Mint
Mentha sp.

Mint sauce with lamb is traditional, but mint can be used in a wide variety of dishes and makes a most attractive garnish. A few chopped mint leaves included in salads give an extra lift, while various tisanes and fruit punches owe much to the clean flavour of mint. The following recipe is an excellent accompaniment for lamb or cold chicken.

Peppermint Jelly
1 kg tart apples
1 tablespoon white wine vinegar
Water
¾ cup sugar for every 425 ml of liquid
1 sprig of peppermint for every 425 ml of liquid

Cut apples into quarters. Do not peel or remove seeds. Barely cover with water and boil until soft. Have ready a bag made of muslin or very fine netting — mosquito netting would be fine. Pour the fruit into the jelly bag and drain into a bowl overnight. Measure the juice. Add the vinegar and mint and boil for 10 minutes. Warm the sugar in the oven and add slowly to the boiling liquid. Stir until sugar is thoroughly dissolved. Boil the jelly until the sugar thermometer registers 100°C. Remove the mint and pour into sterilised and warmed jars. Seal. If wished, fresh peppermint chopped very finely may be added to the jelly before pouring into the jars.

Spearmint Punch
6 large sprigs spearmint
Juice of three oranges
Juice of one large lemon
850 ml cider, chilled
650 ml apple juice
6 tablespoons sugar

Wash the mint, bruise it between the fingers, and put it into a large glass jug.

Pour the juices over the mint and add the sugar, stirring well. Stand for 1 hour and then place in the refrigerator to chill. Prior to serving add cider and pour over crushed ice in a punch bowl. Garnish with fresh sprigs of mint and orange slices.

Minted Pineapple
½ medium sized fresh pineapple or 1 450 g can pineapple
1 tablespoon sugar if using fresh fruit
1 tablespoon brandy
2 sprigs mint for garnishing
1 tablespoon mint, chopped
2 maraschino cherries

If using fresh pineapple, peel, core and dice flesh. If using canned fruit, drain pieces well, reserving liquid for inclusion in fruit drinks. Chop mint finely and place pineapple and mint together in a bowl. Pour over brandy and, if using fresh fruit, sprinkle with sugar. Cover and place in refrigerator for several hours to chill thoroughly and to allow flavour to develop fully. Serve in 2 small dishes, topping each with a cherry and garnish with a mint sprig. This makes a delicious appetiser. If serving only one, the remaining portion will keep in the refrigerator for 4 or 5 days.

Beef and Mint Terrine
1 kg lean minced steak
1 cup fresh breadcrumbs
Salt and freshly ground black pepper
2 tablespoons finely chopped mint leaves
2 beaten eggs
4 rashers bacon, with rind removed
2 onions, finely chopped
½ cup brandy

Chop bacon. Mix all ingredients together and pat mixture into greased terrine or meat loaf tin. Bake for 30–45 minutes in a moderate oven — 190°C. May be eaten hot or served cold with salads. *Serves 6.*

Mugwort
Artemisia vulgare

Related to tarragon, the classic French herb, mugwort has a sprawling growth habit. Only the buds are used for flavouring and on the Continent they are believed to help digest goose, duck, fat meats and fish. It is also used in the distillation of vermouth and absinthe. Mugwort tea was favoured as a treatment for "general body pain" and herbalists still prescribe infusions for, among other things, its diuretic and slightly tonic effects.

Mugwort Tea
1 teaspoon unopened mugwort flower buds, infused in a cup of boiling water for 5 minutes. Strain and serve with a slice of lemon or sweeten with honey. *Serves 1.*

Nasturtium
Tropaeolum majus

Possessing antibiotic qualities, nasturtium is used in some continental countries as a type of herbal penicillin. It has an amazing content of vitamin C. Modern research has found that the vitamin C content is highest in the leaves before July, when nasturtiums generally commence flowering in cool climates. In warmer areas they flower throughout the year. It may be used as a pepper substitute without harming those with ulcers. Sow the nasturtium seed where it is intended to grow this colourful herb.

Nasturtium Sandwiches
Wash and dry well nasturtium leaves and chop finely. Butter whole grain or rye bread and place leaves on the buttered bread. Cover with another buttered slice and cut into fingers. Serve soon after making.

Nasturtium Appetiser
12 nasturtium flowers and 12 leaves
125 g cottage cheese
1 dessertspoon finely chopped chives
¼ teaspoon very finely chopped sage

Pick the nasturtium flowers and leaves before the sun has hit them: Wash them well but gently. Carefully pat dry with paper towels. Mix cheese, chives and sage together very thoroughly. Spoon mixture into the heart of each flower. Arrange the leaves on a serving plate and place a flower on each.

Salad with Nasturtium Dressing
1 washed and dried lettuce torn into bite-size pieces
6 nasturtium flowers washed and dried and torn in pieces
Juice 2 lemons
3 tablespoons olive oil
Salt to taste
1 teaspoon finely chopped chervil
1 dessertspoon finely chopped nasturtium leaves

Place oil together with juice in a small bowl and mix well. Add nasturtium leaves and chervil with salt to taste and mix well. Place lettuce leaves and nasturtium flowers attractively in a glass bowl and pour dressing over. Toss with wooden servers and serve immediately. *Serves 4–6.*

Oregano
Oreganum vulgare

This is a very pungent herb, and one of my favourites. I use the small, grey-green slightly oval leaves extensively in my kitchen and like the flavour in fish, chicken and sausage dishes. I also use it in pâté, and tomato salads. Native to Italy, oregano prefers dry chalky soil and, in common with most herbs, sun.

Mushroom Appetiser
500 g small button mushrooms, fresh
  or canned
2 sprays oregano
Olive oil
½ teaspoon garlic juice

If mushrooms are canned, drain from the brine. Wash and dry fresh mushrooms or drained canned mushrooms and put into a glass jar. Add oregano and garlic juice. Cover with oil and leave for a week before serving the mushrooms, speared on toothpicks, with drinks. The oil may be used in oil and vinegar dressing.

Chicken and Mushrooms
1½ kg chicken pieces
2 teaspoons chopped oregano
2 tablespoons butter or margarine
1 large onion finely chopped
Salt and freshly ground pepper
2 tablespoons plain flour
250 g sliced mushrooms
1 cup dry white wine

Place flour, oregano, salt and pepper in a plastic bag and shake chicken pieces one at a time in the mixture. Melt butter in heavy casserole dish and sauté onion. Add chicken pieces and fry until lightly golden. Remove from heat and add mushrooms, wine and any flour mixture remaining in the bag. Mix well and cover dish. Place in a moderate oven (175°C) and cook for 1½ hours. Serve with jacket baked potatoes. *Serves 6.*

Individual Quiche Lorraines
Prepared shortcrust pastry
125 g bacon
125 g cheddar cheese cut into thin
  slices
1 teaspoon parsley, finely chopped
1 teaspoon oregano
1 small onion, peeled and finely
  chopped
150 ml cream
1 egg
Salt and freshly ground pepper

Line two small pie dishes, about 10 cm in diameter, with shortcrust pastry and prick thoroughly with a fork. Glaze the edges with a little milk. Remove rind from bacon and chop roughly. Fry it in its own fat until crisp. Put cheddar cheese slices on the bottom of each dish and top with half the bacon and onion and sprinkle with oregano. Repeat layers. Beat egg with cream and season with salt and pepper. Add parsley. Pour custard mixture over cheese and bacon layers. Bake in a 190°C oven for about 20 minutes or until set. To check whether cooked, insert a knife in the centre of each quiche. If it comes out clean, the tarts are cooked. This is delicious eaten hot or cold and is a great idea for a picnic. Serve with salad and French bread for a satisfying meal. Quiche will keep in the refrigerator for about 3 days. If wishing to make one large quiche, about 23 cm pie plate size, double the ingredients.

Chicken Liver Pâté

500 g chicken livers
2 slices bacon
1 finely chopped onion
1 tablespoon butter or margarine
2 tablespoons brandy
Salt and freshly ground pepper
½ teaspoon rosemary chopped
2 teaspoons oregano, chopped
Water

Cover chicken livers with water. Add chopped bacon, onion, rosemary and oregano. Cook for approximately 15 minutes. Cool and drain off water. Place chicken mixture in blender or food processor. Add butter or margarine, brandy, salt and pepper. Blend until smooth and pack into small serving dishes or pâté bowls. Serve with triangles of toast. *Serves 6–8.*

Pâté may be frozen if the bowls are covered with heavy duty plastic film. I have done it very successfully many times and it will remain in perfect condition in the freezer for up to 3 weeks.

Parsley

Petroselinum sp.

A hardy biennial, parsley, either triple-curled or Italian, should always be plucked from the outside of the plant as the new, tender growth springs from the centre. Ideal in all manner of savoury dishes, both hot and cold, and as a garnish, this herb is used almost universally. For cooked dishes it is best to add it just prior to the completion of cooking. It combines well with other herbs as the following recipe illustrates.

Green Mayonnaise

2 egg yolks
1 teaspoon sugar
1 teaspoon salt
1 teaspoon Dijon mustard
Freshly ground pepper
1 teaspoon lemon juice
1¼ cups olive oil
3 tablespoons dry white wine
2 teaspoons chopped parsley
1 teaspoon dill, chopped
1 teaspoon chopped chervil
1 teaspoon chopped chives

The blender is useful here for smooth mixing, otherwise, use a rotary beater. At medium speed, blend egg yolks, salt, sugar, mustard, lemon juice and pepper. While blender is in motion, add oil slowly, virtually drop by drop. When all oil is added and the mixture looks milky, add the wine. After the mixture is thick, add the herbs. Chill in covered bowl for 3 hours to permit the flavour to develop. Place in serving dish and top with finely chopped parsley.

Herbed Lamb Chops

2 thick lamb chops
1 dessertspoon finely chopped parsley
1 teaspoon finely chopped marjoram
1 teaspoon finely chopped thyme
Salt and freshly ground pepper
1 dessertspoon butter or margarine
1 beaten egg
1 tablespoon dried breadcrumbs

Mix herbs, butter, salt and pepper to a paste and rub it well into both sides of the chops. Dip each chop into beaten egg and coat thoroughly with breadcrumbs. Grill in usual manner. Serve with sautéed chived potatoes and preferred vegetables. Veal or pork chops are equally delicious prepared this way.

Rose

Rosa sp.

The Elizabethans of Tudor England favoured roses as a flavouring and used them extensively in desserts, sweets and cakes. The smell of a deeply fragrant rose stirs the senses. Imagine Rose Petal Salad being featured at your next dinner party and the sensation it would create! Remember always to choose roses with the strongest perfume for utmost flavour. Rose petals may also be placed in the base of a greased cake tin before the batter is poured in. When the cooked cake is turned out merely peel off the petals.

Rose Petal Salad

*1½ cups rose petals with white bases
   snipped off
1 head each of chicory and lettuce
Rose petal dressing (see below)
1 dessertspoon finely chopped parsley*

Wash and dry the rose petals very gently. The easiest way to dry them is with paper towels. Wash and dry the lettuce and chicory and place in the refrigerator to crisp. Meantime, make the rose dressing using rose vinegar. Place greens, petals and parsley in a glass serving bowl and drizzle dressing over. Toss well and serve immediately. *Serves 6–8.*

Rose Vinegar

*1 cup fresh rose petals packed tightly
850 ml white wine or cider vinegar*

Wash and dry rose petals and place them in a large screw-top jar. Pour the vinegar over and stand on a sunny window for 3 weeks, tightly sealed, then strain through a very fine sieve and discard petals. Pour strained vinegar into capped bottles.

Rose Dressing

*3 tablespoons peanut oil
2 tablespoons rose vinegar
Salt and freshly ground pepper*

Mix all ingredients in a screw-top jar and shake well.

Rose Hip Soup

*2 cups water
1 cup rose hips
1 extra tablespoon water
½ tablespoon cornflour or 1 medium
   potato, grated
Salt and freshly ground pepper to taste
2 tablespoons madeira or sweet sherry
1 dessertspoon toasted and finely
   chopped almonds*

Place rose hips and 2 cups of water in a saucepan and cook gently for 1–2 hours or until tender. Place in blender and whirr until smooth. Measure three-quarters to one cup of blended mixture, adding more water if necessary. Reheat. Mix 1 table-spoon water and ½ tablespoon cornflour or grated potato and add to rose hip mixture and stir until smooth and thick. Add salt and pepper to taste, and madeira. Place in ramekins and top with chopped almonds. *Serves 2.*

Rose Cordial

*10 g sugar
850 ml good quality brandy
1 cup washed and dried rose petals
1 large sterilised jar with a lid*

Place brandy, sugar and rose petals in the jar and stand in a cool dark place for 2 months. Shake jar occasionally. When ready pour the cordial through a sieve or filter. Discard the rose petals. Rebottle, cork and serve at room temperature after dinner. Yields 850 ml of cordial.

Rosemary
Rosmarinus officinalis

Rosemary is an extremely versatile herb and adds piquancy to casseroles, stews and chicken dishes. Scones flavoured with rosemary are delicious and very simple to make. Rosemary has a strong flavour so use discreetly.

Rosemary Scones
2 cups plain flour
1 teaspoon baking powder
¼ teaspoon each salt and sugar
1 tablespoon butter or margarine
1 tablespoon finely chopped rosemary
275 ml milk

Sift flour, baking powder, salt and sugar. Rub in the butter or margarine, add the rosemary and milk. Mix to a soft dough, roll lightly and cut into rounds. Place rounds on a greased baking sheet dusted with flour and bake in a hot oven (210°C) for about 15 minutes. The scones may be served, buttered, either hot or cold. *Yields about 1 dozen.*

Rosemary Chops
4 thick lamb chops (preferably short loin)
1 teaspoon chopped rosemary
2 teaspoons butter or margarine
½ crushed clove of garlic
2 teaspoons chopped chives
1 extra tablespoon butter or margarine, melted

Mix rosemary and garlic into butter or margarine, blending well. Make a slit in each chop and insert some of the mixture. Grill in usual manner for approximately 10 minutes on each side or until done to preference. Pour melted butter or margarine containing chives over chops and serve immediately with selected vegetables. *Serves 4.*

Tomato Sauce
1½ cups vegetable stock
750 g fresh or canned tomatoes
1 large onion finely chopped
4 tablespoons melted butter
1 bouquet garni consisting of a sprig of rosemary, another of thyme, 1 bay leaf and a spray of basil
Salt and freshly ground pepper
1 teaspoon sugar
1 tablespoon cornflour
2 tablespoons milk

Chop peeled tomatoes into small pieces and place them in a pan with onions and melted butter. Cook in tightly lidded pan for 10 minutes over gentle heat, shaking occasionally. Add herbs, stock, salt, pepper and sugar. (For easy removal, the herbs should be tied together with white string and suspended from the pan's handle.) The sugar counteracts the acidity of the tomatoes. Cook very slowly for half an hour, stirring from time to time with a wooden spoon. Puree in a blender or food processor or strain through a coarse sieve. Return mixture to the pan and bring to the boil. Blend cornflour into the milk and stir into tomato mixture slowly. Bring pan contents to the boil, stirring constantly. Remove herbs. Cook for a further 5 minutes and check seasonings before serving with pasta or fish.

Rosemary Beef Stew
500 g stewing beef
125 g bacon, or 4 slices
Salt and freshly ground pepper
1 tablespoon flour
1 dessertspoon oil
1 dessertspoon butter or margarine
1 clove garlic, chopped finely or
*   crushed*
1 teaspoon rosemary, chopped finely
1 cup stock or water
½ teaspoon finely chopped sage
1 large carrot scraped and cut into
*   slices*
1 cup red wine
1 onion peeled and sliced

Cut meat into 4 serving sized pieces, removing fat. Take rind off the bacon and wrap a rasher around each piece of meat. Secure with tooth picks, which should be removed before serving. Mix salt and pepper with flour and coat meat pieces. Drip a little oil on each piece. Melt butter or margarine in a pan and brown meat on all sides. Remove from the pan and place in a casserole with onion, carrot, garlic, rosemary and sage. Pour over stock or water, cover and simmer in a slow (85°C) oven for 2 hours. Add wine and stew gently for another hour. If desired, remaining gravy may be thickened with a little cornflour. Serve with noodles, or potatoes which have been wrapped in foil and baked. If only 1 serving is required, remaining meat and vegetables may be frozen.

Coq au Vin
1 kg chicken pieces
2 tablespoons flour
Salt and freshly ground pepper
½ cup red wine
1 tablespoon brandy
1 teaspoon thyme
1 teaspoon rosemary
1 onion peeled and finely chopped
250 g peeled and chopped tomatoes,
*   fresh or canned*
3 slices bacon with rind removed
3 tablespoons butter
½ cup water

Chop bacon and sauté gently in its own fat. Place flour, salt and pepper in a plastic bag and dredge chicken pieces. Remove bacon from pan and retaining fat add butter and melt. Do not brown. Add chicken pieces, a few at a time and sauté both sides until golden. Remove and place with bacon in an ovenproof dish. Sauté onions in pan and add to the casserole. Add tomatoes, herbs, red wine and water. Warm brandy and ignite and pour over the contents of casserole while still flaming. Cover and place in moderate oven (190°C) and bake for 1½ hours approximately. Serve with potatoes wrapped in foil and oven baked. *Serves 4.*

Rue
Ruta graveolens

The seed is slow in germination and the plant in growth habit, so it takes some time for this herb to attain its ultimate height of approximately 40 cm. Rue tea is regarded medically as a stimulant and anti-spasmodic. It has little other culinary value, however, though in some parts of Scotland it is sometimes used sparingly on sandwiches.

Rue Tea
1 teaspoon rue leaves
1 tablespoon honey
1 cup boiling water

Infuse the leaves in the boiling water for 5 minutes. Strain and sweeten with honey. Rue tea is bitter, hence the large quantity of honey. *Serves 1.*

Sage
Salvia officinalis

This is the better known sage, although *Salvia rutans*, the pineapple sage, is gaining popularity. The salvia family is a large one, although most members of it are grown for ornamental purposes. Sage is a must in dishes including fat meats such as pork, or fish such as eel, as this pungent herb renders these meats more digestible. It is also excellent with cheeses. Many people throughout Europe use dried sage leaves as a tooth powder to whiten teeth and to remove stains. Quite a boon for the heavy smoker!

Sage Cheese Spread
1 cup cottage or creamed cheese
Juice 1 lemon
1 dessertspoon finely chopped sage
1 teaspoon finely chopped chives
Freshly ground pepper

Beat all ingredients thoroughly and place in lidded container. Store in the refrigerator. This is delicious spread on crackers or canapes. Alternatively, it may be formed into a ball and rolled in crushed nuts. Serve individual balls with small green salads instead of the usual cheese platter. Accompany with crackers. *Yields about 6 balls.*

Sage Potatoes
1 kg peeled and boiled potatoes, diced
2 tablespoons butter or margarine
2 teaspoons finely chopped sage
½ teaspoon finely chopped parsley
1 teaspoon finely chopped chives
125 g Philadelphia cream cheese
¼ cup milk

Melt butter or margarine and sauté potatoes until golden. Add herbs and sauté again. Place in a well greased casserole dish. Mix milk and cheese well and pour over the potatoes. Bake in 175°C oven for about an hour or until golden. *Serves 6.*

Nasturtium provides glorious colour in the garden
and gives bite to salads.

An alfresco meal of herb punch, minted pineapple,
chicken with mushrooms, and tossed salad with balm.

Sage and Onion Seasoning (for all poultry or pork)
6 small onions
3 teaspoons butter or margarine
¾ cup milk
½ cup fresh breadcrumbs
1 dessertspoon finely chopped parsley
1 tablespoon finely chopped sage
  leaves
Salt and freshly ground pepper

Peel and chop onions roughly and boil in the milk until half cooked. Add the butter or margarine and allow to melt in milk and onion mixture. Add the breadcrumbs, which will absorb the milk, sprinkle in the parsley, sage, salt and pepper and mix thoroughly. Stuff poultry or pork with seasoning. When cold this retains its moisture and adds delicious flavour to cold poultry or pork sandwiches.

Saltimbocca
4 thin slices veal, pounded until thin
  between 2 sheets of waxed paper
4 thin slices prosciutto or smoked ham
8 sage leaves
1 tablespoon butter
1 cup dry white wine
Salt and freshly ground pepper
1 tablespoon flour

Place ham on veal slices and top each piece with 2 sage leaves. Roll up and secure with tooth picks. Add salt and pepper to flour and coat rolls. Melt butter in pan and fry meat until golden brown. Add wine and cover pan, simmering gently until meat is tender.

Santolina
Santolina chamaecyparissus

This silvery leafed herb was originally cultivated for its pungency and appearance. Later its insect repelling qualities were discovered as were those of rosemary, mint, etc. Sometimes referred to as the "cotton lavender" santolina was first introduced into Great Britain in 1573 from southern Europe.

  Experiment showed this herb to be as interesting an addition to pork and fatty fish as sage, both herbs rendering such foods more digestible. Try sprinkling some finely chopped leaves onto pork chops prior to grilling or baking.

Bulghur Pilaf
3 tablespoons bulghur (cracked wheat)
1 tablespoon butter or margarine
2 tablespoons peeled and finely diced
  onion
¼ teaspoon finely chopped oregano
125 g finely diced prosciutto or ham
1 small cup tuna, well drained
½ cup santolina beef stock (see below)
Salt and freshly ground pepper
1 tablespoon parsley, chopped
1 dessertspoon snipped chives
1 teaspoon paprika (optional)
2 lemon wedges

To make santolina beef stock, infuse a sprig of santolina in hot beef stock for 15 minutes and then strain. Sauté bulghur, onion and oregano in melted butter or margarine until onion is golden. Add stock, salt and freshly ground pepper. Bring slowly to the boil and continue to cook over low heat until liquid is absorbed and bulghur is fluffy. Add ham, tuna (flaked with a fork) and parsley and heat through. Spoon into a heated serving dish and garnish with lemon wedges and sprinkle with chives and paprika, if used.

Santolina Pork Fillet

1 kg pork fillet
1-1½ cups grated onion
2 crushed cloves garlic
Juice and pulped fruit of 1 large orange
*   or 2 mandarins*
Juice and pulped fruit of 1 large lemon
*   or of 2 limes if available*
4 medium sized sprays of santolina
*   finely chopped (Do not use stems as*
*   they are a little woody)*
4 tablespoons oil
2 tablespoons dry white wine,
*   combined with an equal amount of*
*   water*
3 additional sprays of santolina
½ cup cream

Combine the garlic, juice, chopped onion and santolina and marinate fillet in mixture standing for 6 hours, during which time meat should be turned frequently. Using a broad bladed knife, scrape off any adhering marinade and carefully sear pork in four tablespoons of hot oil. When sealed on all sides transfer the fillet into a roasting dish and deglaze pan with 2 tablespoons of dry white wine combined with 2 tablespoons water.

Pour liquid over meat and on top place additional santolina sprays. Roast in a medium oven basting frequently with pan juices for an hour or until no "pink" shows when tested with a fork or skewer. If necessary, add more wine and water mixture. Discard santolina sprays and blend dish juices with ½ cup cream. Heat thoroughly but do not boil. Pour over pork and serve immediately.

Savory
Satureia sp.

I prefer winter savory to the slightly milder annual summer savory. It has a strong, biting flavour and makes an excellent pepper substitute for those on diets precluding the use of the pungent seasoning. The Romans made a savory sauce which was used with meats much as we use mint sauce today. If a leaf is boiled with cabbage, cauliflower or brussels sprouts, there will be no unpleasant odour. It should, however, be used with restraint. The prostrate winter savory is also useful in the kitchen.

Savory Baked Fish with Cider

1 kg filleted fish
2 peeled and cored apples, cut into
*   eighths*
1 stick celery thinly sliced
1 carrot thinly sliced
3 finely chopped shallots or two
*   chopped spring onions*
¾ cup cider
¼ cup fresh breadcrumbs
1 teaspoon butter or margarine
1 tablespoon finely chopped savory
Salt and freshly ground pepper
2 tablespoons plain flour

Roll fillets in flour and put them in a buttered casserole dish with vegetables, apple and savory. Add salt and pepper. Pour in cider very carefully. Fry breadcrumbs in butter or margarine and sprinkle on top of dish. Bake, uncovered, in a 175°C oven for 20–30 minutes.

Surprise Herbed Eggs

2 eggs
1 tablespoon mayonnaise
2 teaspoons tarragon, finely chopped
2 teaspoons finely chopped parsley
Salt and freshly ground pepper
1 100 g can sardines drained of oil
1 teaspoon curry powder
Freshly ground pepper (optional)
2 lettuce leaves

Hard boil eggs for 10 minutes. Shell and cut into halves. Gently remove yolks and place in a small bowl. Mash well and add mashed sardines, tarragon and parsley. Combine and blend well mayonnaise, curry powder and pepper if used. Add to egg and sardine mixture and mix very well. Heap into egg white halves and serve 2 on each lettuce leaf as an appetiser.

Herbed Chicken

1 x 2½ kg chicken, boned
3 tablespoons melted butter or
    margarine
½ cup red currant jelly
Salt and freshly ground black pepper

Stuffing

1 cup soft breadcrumbs
1 lightly beaten egg
1 teaspoon finely chopped savory
1 teaspoon finely chopped parsley
1 teaspoon finely chopped thyme
Grated rind of lemon
Oil

Ask your butcher to bone the chicken — it's much simpler that way! Fold the egg into the breadcrumbs and add herbs and grated lemon rind. Moisten further with melted butter or margarine and season with salt and pepper. Put the bird on a board with the skin down and spread with the mixture. Roll up and tie with white string along the length of the roll. Heat oil in baking dish and bake chicken for approximately 2½ hours or until done, basting frequently with pan drippings.

When cooked, remove from the dish and cool. Remove strings and transfer to a large serving platter. Glaze with red-currant jelly and garnish with thinly sliced lemon and sprigs of parsley. This is an ideal dish for a cold buffet and should serve 6.

Ratatouille

500 g courgettes (zucchini)
1 aubergine (eggplant)
250 g fresh or drained canned tomatoes
1 large red pepper
1 large green pepper
2 small white onions peeled and finely
    sliced into rings
1 clove garlic finely chopped
1 dessertspoon winter savory finely
    chopped
4 tablespoons olive oil
Salt and freshly ground pepper

Slice courgettes and aubergine and place in a dish together. Salt and leave for half an hour. Remove skin from fresh tomatoes, or drain canned ones, and chop. Halve the peppers and carefully scrape out seeds from shells. Discard seeds and shred peppers finely. Melt oil in heavy frying pan and lightly fry onions and garlic for 2 minutes. Drain courgettes and aubergine and pat dry. Add to pan and gently sauté for 2 minutes on each side. Add extra oil if needed. Season with salt and freshly ground black pepper and add savory. Add tomatoes and peppers. Bake for 1 hour in a covered casserole in a 175°C oven. The vegetables will cook down into a rich mass. This is excellent with chicken, fish or hamburger patties. Serves 6–8.

Savory Bean Salad

1 440 g can mixed beans
1 peeled and finely chopped small
 onion
1 piece celery about 12 cm long, sliced
 thinly
1 teaspoon finely chopped savory
1 teaspoon capers
1 small grated carrot
Judith's Dressing (see Green Balm
 Salad)

Drain beans and wash well under running water to remove any remaining liquid. Combine with all other ingredients and toss well to mix. Place in a covered container in the refrigerator and chill well. Serve with cold meats or with barbecues. Will keep under refrigeration for about 5 days.

Tansy
Tanacetum vulgare

Rarely used these days in the kitchen, centuries ago tansy was used to flavour various "puddings" ranging from a type of dough cake to a mousse-like confection of eggs, sugar and cream.

Tansy Cake

1 cold baked 23 cm pie shell
2½ cups cream
7 eggs
10 tansy leaves (to make 1 teaspoon of
 juice)
6 large spinach leaves (to make 1
 dessertspoon of juice)
White wine, sugar and nutmeg to taste

Place tansy and spinach leaves separately in a juice extractor, or pound, separately, with a pestle in a mortar. Measure juice and set aside. Beat eggs very well and blend in cream thoroughly. Add tansy juice to flavour the mixture and spinach juice to colour it. When juices are thoroughly blended, slowly add wine, sugar and nutmeg until the taste suits your palate. Warm the mixture gently in a saucepan until it is thick. Cool slightly and pour into the pie shell. Let the pudding stand until it sets and serve cold.

Tarragon
Artemisia dracunculus

Tarragon is one of the most aristocratic herbs. Immortalised in such sauces as béarnaise and hollandaise and in tarragon vinegar, this elusively pungent herb is highly prized by French chefs and this variety is in fact referred to as French tarragon.

Tarragon Vinegar
In a glass jar place tender young shoots of tarragon. Pour wine vinegar over them and cover tightly. After infusing for 2 weeks strain through a fine sieve or a piece of fine nylon material and pour into sterilised bottles. A fresh spray of tarragon added to each bottle will look decorative and continue to add strength to the vinegar.

Avocado and Crab Mousse
2 avocados, peeled, diced and
    sprinkled with lemon juice to
    prevent discolouration
2 cups crab meat, fresh or canned
1 cup finely diced celery
1 850 ml can undiluted tomato juice
1 tablespoon chopped tarragon
1½ tablespoons gelatine
Salt and freshly ground black pepper

Soak gelatine in ½ cup of heated tomato juice for 5 minutes. In the meantime, blend avocado, crab meat, tarragon and celery. Add salt and pepper to taste. Stir remaining juice slowly into the gelatine mixture and then add this to the crab meat and set in an oiled mould. When firm, turn out onto a bed of watercress or parsley. Garnish with finely cut slices of lemon and, if wished, cucumber sliced thinly and sprinkled with dill.

Wined Chicken Liver Appetiser
750 g chicken livers
250 ml dry white wine such as chablis
2 teaspoons finely chopped tarragon
125 g butter or margarine
2 cloves garlic, finely diced or crushed
2 teaspoons marjoram
1 tablespoon plain flour
Salt and freshly ground pepper

Wash the chicken livers well and cut into halves. Simmer gently with the garlic in the butter or margarine for about 15 minutes. Add herbs and flour, seasoning with salt and pepper. Toss livers until flour browns slightly. Blend all well, slowly adding the wine. Stir until sauce is thick and smooth. Serve with boiled rice or buttered noodles. *Serves 8. If preferred as a luncheon or supper course, this will serve 4.*

Thyme
Thymus sp.

This is a herb which, in its different varieties with their wide range of flavours, adds zest to many types of fish, fowl, meat and vegetable dishes. It is almost indispensable in the kitchen and has proven itself through the ages in the medicinal field.

Mushrooms with Thyme
500 g washed and sliced mushrooms
½ cup thickened cream
1 tablespoon vermouth or dry sherry
Salt and freshly ground black pepper
1 dessertspoon thyme
1 tablespoon flour
1 tablespoon butter

Make a roux of butter and flour and gradually add cream, stirring until smooth. Add mushrooms, vermouth, thyme, salt and pepper. Simmer for 10 minutes over low heat, stirring occasionally to prevent sticking. If too thick, add a little milk. Lemon thyme is quite good in this dish.

Rabbit in Red Wine
1 rabbit cut into pieces
2 tablespoons plain flour
1 small cup oil
2 finely chopped medium onions
1 cup red wine
½ cup water
Salt and freshly ground black pepper
2 tablespoons chopped thyme

Roll rabbit pieces in flour. Heating the oil in a heavy pan, fry the floured pieces gently until golden brown. Layer rabbit, thyme and onions in a casserole dish adding salt and pepper to each layer. Pour over wine and water. Cover and bake in a 175°C oven for 2 hours or until rabbit is tender when pierced with a fork or skewer.

Meat Balls in Wine Sauce
1 cup red wine
850 ml beef stock
1 onion, left whole
1 bay leaf
6 black peppercorns
¼ teaspoon salt
1 dessertspoon cornflour
1 tablespoon finely chopped parsley

Simmer above ingredients (except cornflour and parsley) together for 15 minutes and remove onion and bay leaf. Put sauce to one side.

750 g lean minced steak
1 beaten egg
1 finely chopped onion
2 teaspoons thyme
Salt and freshly ground pepper

Mix above meat ball ingredients and with wet hands form the meat mixture into small balls and simmer for 30 minutes. Remove meat balls and keep them warm. Using one dessertspoon cornflour blended in a little water, thicken the sauce. Stir until smooth and add one tablespoon finely chopped parsley. Pour sauce over meat balls and serve hot with buttered noodles. *Serves 6.*

Thyme Meat Loaf

125 g very finely diced or minced
* bacon or prosciutto*
250 g good quality lean minced steak
½ cup milk
Salt and freshly ground pepper
2 tablespoons soft breadcrumbs
1 small egg
1 small finely chopped onion
1 dessertspoon chopped thyme
2 hard-boiled eggs, shelled and sliced

Place minced beef and bacon in a mixing bowl with crumbs, thyme, onion, salt and pepper. With a fork or wet hands work all together well and add the milk and egg, mixing all together. Place half the mixture in a small loaf tin and top with sliced hard-boiled eggs. Cover with remaining meat mixture. Bake in a 190°C oven for three-quarters of an hour or until cooked. This keeps quite well so you may wish to double all quantities other than hard-boiled eggs. It is delicious hot or cold.

Violet
Viola sp.

The sweet perfume and dainty flowers of violets have endeared them to everyone through the ages. Used for decoration, cosmetics, perfume and dyeing, they also have a place in the kitchen. Gather the blooms before they are hit by the sun, wash them gently and carefully pat dry with paper towels. When crystallised, they add delightful decoration to cakes and desserts.

Crystallised Violets

1 large bunch of violet flowers with all
* green removed carefully*
2 egg whites
250 g castor sugar
¼ teaspoon violet extract or purple
* food colouring*

Beat egg whites until thick and foamy but *not* stiff. Add a few drops of food colouring and dip each flower separately until thoroughly coated, then dip into sugar, making sure all sides are covered. Place on greaseproof paper to dry, using a tooth pick to open each flower to its fullest. Keep flowers a little distance from each other and dry in a warm place. Store dried and candied violets in an airtight tin. These may be passed with coffee or used as a decoration for cakes or sweets. According to bunch size, this should yield about 6 dozen.

Exotic Omelette avec Violets

1 teaspoon butter or margarine
4 eggs
1 tablespoon water
10 violet leaves
10 violet flowers with all white parts
removed
Salt and freshly ground pepper
1 teaspoon parsley or chervil, finely
chopped (optional)

Wash violet flowers and leaves and pat dry with paper towels. Place in refrigerator to crisp. Whisk eggs until frothy and golden. Add water, salt and pepper. Melt butter or margarine in a pan. Pour in egg mixture and using a knife or spatula cut around edges of omelette and lightly score across the middle until top of mixture is bubbly. Chop violet leaves and sprinkle on top with parsley or chervil if used. Fold omelette in half and cook for a few minutes longer. Serve immediately, garnished with violet flowers, on warmed plates.

Violet Bombe

1 litre carton vanilla icecream
250 g thickened cream flavoured with a
tablespoon brandy
4 crystallised violets or fresh violets

Scoop icecream into four tall, or sundae, glasses and pipe cream over each scoop, forming rosettes. Centre each rosette with a violet. *Serves 4.* It is necessary to work quickly. It would be a help to have the glasses well chilled and place each in freezer until all four are completed and ready to serve.

Violet Salad

2 shelled and chopped hard boiled eggs.
2 tablespoons croutons
1 bunch watercress
1 medium lettuce
1 teaspoon white wine vinegar
3 teaspoons olive oil
Salt and freshly ground pepper
1 cup violet flowers crisped in ice
water and patted dry

Wash watercress and lettuce and shake until dry. Remove all green parts from violets. Mix oil, vinegar, salt and pepper in a lidded jar and shake well. Tear lettuce into bite-size pieces and place in a glass dish with chopped eggs and watercress. Pouring over dressing, toss until leaves are well coated. Add violet flowers and croutons and turn over once or twice. *Serves 6.*

Watercress
Nasturtium officinale

Delicious as a salad with a vinegar and oil dressing, watercress also combines well with other salad greens. This sauce is a delightful accompaniment to sausages or cold and hot roast meats. It also goes well when served cold with hard boiled eggs.

Watercress Sauce

2 tablespoons butter or margarine
2 tablespoons flour
2 scant cups milk
3 tablespoons watercress
¼ teaspoon salt

Melt butter or margarine and add flour, making a roux. Add milk gradually, stirring well. Season with salt and toss in washed, dried and chopped watercress. Stir for one minute longer.

HERBAL BEAUTY
7

Herbal beauty products are pure, fresh and inexpensive. Simple to prepare, they offer many benefits. Herbs can be used in a daily beauty care programme, in steam baths, face washes, eye baths, hair rinses, face packs and herbal baths, the last helping to relax tired muscles and tone the skin.

It is important to remember that beauty *does* come from within. A slogan which intrigued me as a child was above a bakery: "What we eat today, walks and talks tomorrow." Herbs added to our regular meals and herbal teas all help to cleanse and purify our bodies and complexions and invigorate us. All this helps us to face the daily stresses and strains of modern day living.

Herbal Baths

The most simple way to use herbs in a beauty programme is in a herbal bath. Any number of herbs may be added to the running water, either singly or in a combination. Eau-de-cologne mint, lovage, camomile blooms, rosemary, sage, rose petals and fennel are all effective. The natural oils released by the hot water are most beneficial to the skin, and the savings compared with the cost of commercially prepared bath additives are quite considerable.

Herbal steam baths open the skin and release the impurities trapped in the pores. Herbal face packs will help to fade freckles and dark pigmentation marks. If the skin is particularly dry don't use a steam bath, but instead splash a wash on the face to help cleanse and impart a youthful glow.

Herbs useful in the steam bath are camomile flowers, marigold (*Calendula officinalis*) peppermint, sage, elderflower, yarrow, lavender flowers, salad burnet and nasturtium flowers. These may be used in any combination of equal quantities or singly.

Face Cleansers and Packs

To take advantage of the steam bath, first cleanse the face well and tie back the hair.

Place half a cup of the chosen herb or herbs in a large china bowl and pour 600 ml of boiling water over them. Cover your head with a large towel and bend over the bowl, covering the bowl also with the towel to form a "tent", and bringing your face about 20 cm from the bowl. Remain covered for approximately ten minutes, then sponge your face with cooled lavender or rose water. Remain indoors, to allow your system to adjust, for approximately one hour. This treatment may be used once a week to clear the skin of impurities. While your face is freshly clean, a follow up with a face pack is recommended.

Yoghurt or sour cream are both excellent bases into which to blend the chosen herb. Yarrow or camomile will help to cleanse a greasy skin, while fennel will aid a wrinkled skin. Gently stroke on the pack but avoid the delicate eye and mouth areas. Brew an infusion of elderberry or fennel tea and soak two cotton wool pads in this and, lying down with the feet elevated, apply the pads to closed eyes and relax for at least twenty minutes. Soothing background music will provide a calming atmosphere which will make the work of the face pack and eye pads even more effective. Splash off the mask with warm water and tone with cold camomile tea applied to the face with cotton balls or tissues, and gently pat dry.

Dry skin will benefit from a pack made by incorporating ten drops of olive oil, a few drops of lemon juice and one dessertspoon of finely chopped fennel into a beaten egg yolk. This should be left on for twenty minutes and sponged off with fennel tea, slightly warmed.

Oily skin may be treated with a pack made of beaten egg white with six drops of lemon juice added, together with one dessertspoon of finely chopped yarrow. Spread evenly over the face and leave for ten minutes, after which time it should be sponged off with yarrow tea.

Even older skins will benefit from herbal packs. A suitable one may be made from yoghurt, into which has been beaten four tablespoons of finely chopped fennel. This softens the skin and assists in smoothing out wrinkles. Remove the pack with cool water after about fifteen minutes and tone by splashing the face with cold yarrow tea. Pat dry very gently. Remember, with all face packs, to protect the delicate eye area and remember also not to move the facial muscles while the pack is on.

Hand Creams

Hand-cream packs may also be made using herbs to whiten and soften the skin. Once again yoghurt comes into its own with the addition of a strong infusion of camomile together with lemon or cucumber juice and a dessertspoon of honey. Beat all ingredients together well. The honey will have a softening and nourishing effect.

A jar of unscented cold cream is simply made into herbal cream with the addition of finely chopped fennel or elderflower beaten in thoroughly. Herbal oil for dry skins is made by adding chopped rosemary, lemon balm, lavender or lemon verbena to one tablespoon of wine vinegar. Add to a 600 ml bottle that has been three-quarters filled with olive oil. Cork the bottle tightly. Place the bottle on a sunny window sill or shelf and twice a day for about three weeks shake the bottle vigorously. It must have full exposure to sunlight to draw out the full essence of the herbs. At the end of this time, strain the oil into a clean jug and press any remaining oil from the herbs. Repeat the process until when you rub a little oil on the inside of the wrist the fragrance lingers for several minutes. Then you know the oil is of the proper strength. For a decorative effect and to add further fragrance to the herbal oil, add a fresh spray of the chosen herb to the bottle when the oil is finally brewed. Obviously summer, with its long hours of sunlight, is the better time to make herbal oils, which make appreciated gifts. To really dress up the bottle if intended as a gift, tie an appropriately coloured ribbon, for example mauve for lavender oil and soft yellow for lemon verbena or balm, around the neck of the bottle and tuck in a spray of the herb used. If, however, you wish to prepare the oil in winter or during dull weather, it is possible to extract the volatile oils by heating the tightly corked bottles in a deep boiler of water at a little below boiling point for three or four hours daily, over a period of a week.

Eye Lotion

A beneficial lotion for eyes that have become reddened and irritated by wind, late nights, colds or dust, may be made from an infusion of camomile, fennel or elderflower. Add one teaspoon of dried or three teaspoons of fresh herb to a cup of boiling water and let it stand until cool. Strain and, using an eye-glass, bathe away the irritations.

Appetite Suppressant

Fennel has the reputation of aiding those trying to lose weight. A cup of fennel tea, made from either foliage or seeds, using a teaspoonful of either in a cup of boiling water and strained, should be taken each day prior to breakfast and retiring at night. If you feel hunger pangs during the day, try chewing a few fennel or dill seeds.

Hair Rinse

Dandruff may be treated by rubbing an infusion of parsley tea into the scalp every three or four days, and cold sage tea used as a final rinse will, if used regularly, slow down the appearance of grey hairs. Many Italian women make great use of sage rinses with beneficial results. Lavender rinses not only add delightful fragrance to the hair, but also add a rich sheen to any coloured tresses. Make the infusions in the same manner as for eye lotion, but quadruple the quantities. Any of the creams and lotions described would make acceptable and unusual gifts, or could be sold at charity stalls. Choose attractive containers, label carefully with details of ingredients and directions for use, and decorate with ribbons or pretty lace edgings. Remember to keep the look of an article "Olde Worlde", as this is in keeping with herbal products.

Herbal Teas

Herbal teas are not only relaxing, but will also help to clear the skin and give it a healthy glow. Some of these teas, when cooled, may be used as skin washes or hair rinses with great benefit. Camomile and elderflower tea are two examples of teas that will help purify and clean dull, tired skins.

HERBAL GIFTS
8

A fragrant home is always a pleasure to enter and in spite of today's modern chemical "air fresheners" there is none as appealing as the perfume of a bowl of potpourri, potpourri gathered from your own garden or which has been lovingly and carefully prepared by a friend or relation. The magical combination of dried flower petals, herbs, spices, and so on, will not only act as a special pick-me-up to jaded senses, but will also cleanse a room of musty odours, particularly that of heavy tobacco smoke. It is a fine idea after a party, and before retiring, to open a jar of potpourri, stir it lightly with a finger and leave to cleanse the air. On re-entering the room the next morning it will be a surprise to find how much fresher the air is.

Potpourri

Potpourri is fairly easy to make and the ingredients simple to prepare. In chapter 5 you will find directions for drying herbs and flowers. Below are the potpourri ingredients. It is wise to include "fixatives" which are exactly what the name implies — they fix the scent of the ingredients so that the perfume lingers on, even for years!

Dried Flowers and Petals

These will provide colour which is so much of the pleasure of the mixture. They are not so fragrant themselves as others I'll list later, but do add texture as well as hue. Select from any of the following: delphiniums, pansies, larkspur, clematis, marigolds, forget-me-nots, small rosebuds which will shrink and dry into exquisite miniatures, zinnias and camomile flowers.

Perfumed Flowers

Roses head the list as for centuries they have been prized for their delightful perfume. Lavender, carnations, dianthus, jasmine, orange, lemon and lime blossoms, violets, wallflowers, mignonette, lemon verbena flowers, lily-of-the-valley, sweet peas, stocks and jonquils may all be dried

and set aside, not only for potpourri, but also for use in various other joyful delights, such as sachets.

Herbs and Spices

These also play their part, as do the dried and powdered rinds of citrus fruits. Among the herbs most commonly used are marjoram, rosemary, lemon verbena, balm, assorted perfumed geranium leaves, peppermint, lemon and caraway thymes and sweet basil. Spices which may be purchased from various shops include cloves, cinnamon, allspice, nutmeg, coriander seeds and ginger.

Fixatives

Those that are most commonly used are orris root powder and gum benzoin, which should be fairly easy to obtain from pharmacies. There are fragrances which also make acceptable fixatives, but they are fairly expensive and include myrrh, sandalwood and patchouli.

Having resolved to make potpourri, decide which type of container to use. This can be almost anything! Apothecary or coffee jars, glass urns with lids, cosmetic bowls, jam, honey or sugar bowls with lids are all acceptable. If using coffee jars, cover the lids with scraps of flowered print to follow through the theme. When presenting a jar as a gift, attach a printed card listing the main ingredients. For example, "Rose Potpourri", "Lemon Potpourri", "Jasmine Potpourri", and so on.

The potpourri mixture may also be encased in sachets or herbal pillows. The pillows make appreciated gifts for invalids or those who suffer from insomnia, as they gently encourage sleep.

Various oils may also be added to the dried petals and leaves to give extra strength. Some of these are essence of rose, lemon verbena, violet, rosemary, lavender and sandalwood. Salt is always used as a preservative in dry potpourri and also adds bulk.

The proportions for an aromatic mixture are one cup of salt to three cups of fresh petals. Spices should be added at the rate of one tablespoon to four cups of dried petals, and fixatives, according to the strength of perfume in the dried petals and foliage, are added in the proportion of one-third of a cup to between four and eight cups of flower and herb mixture. The oils if used are limited to four or six drops between six to eight cups of the mixture.

There are many methods of making potpourri. The following is an original moist method.

Rose Potpourri

Probably the best-loved potpourri in days past was the rose mixture. Being large, the flowers could be gathered fairly quickly and in quantity. This recipe uses the moist method.

8 cups moist dried rose petals (red for preference, as they are usually the most fragrant)
¾ cup sea salt
¾ cup table salt
⅔ cup orris root powder
2 tablespoons ground mace
2 tablespoons ground nutmeg
2 tablespoons ground allspice
2 tablespoons ground cloves
1 stick cinnamon, crushed
1 cup dried rose buds
4 drops rose oil (usually obtainable from pharmacies)

Combine salts and layer in a 2½ litre jar alternately with rose petals. Place the container in a well-ventilated place for 10 days. Stir mixture daily and when crisp to the touch add the other ingredients. The rose oil should be added a drop at a time and mixed thoroughly into the other ingredients. Allow the potpourri to "ferment" for 6 weeks in an airtight jar. Transfer the mixture then into chosen lidded containers. If wished, a quarter of a cup of powdered ginger could provide variation on this basic recipe.

Simple Mixed Potpourri

3 cups assorted perfumed flower petals
1 cup sea salt
½ tablespoon ground cloves
½ tablespoon ground allspice
½ cup orris root powder
6 drops rose oil

Dry flower petals until they feel leathery. In a large deep bowl place alternate layers of petals and salt, filling it to about two-thirds full. Stand the bowl in a dry, well-aired place for ten days. The petals will be ready as the basis for the potpourri when they have caked together. Break apart the caked petals and add remaining dry ingredients. Place in an airtight container and store for six weeks. Stir frequently in this "fermenting" period. At the end of this time, add the rose oil and seal the container and "ferment" for a further two weeks. Divide into smaller airtight containers.

Carnation Potpourri

This recipe follows the dry method of preparation.

2 cups pink carnation petals
2 cups pink rose petals
½ cup orris root powder
1 whole cinnamon stick, crushed
1 tablespoon ground cinnamon
4 drops rose oil
12 cloves

Dry rose and carnation petals separately. When crisp, combine them in a large dish. Reserve a tablespoon of the orris root powder and sprinkle the remainder over the petals. In a small bowl combine the rose oil and reserved orris powder. Mix until oil is fully absorbed. Sprinkle the cinnamon over petals and stir in the orris root and rose oil mixture. Add the crushed cinnamon stick and cloves. Turn over several times with dry hands. Place in a covered jar and stand for 6 weeks before placing in selected containers.

Lavender Potpourri

2 cups dried lavender flowers
4 tablespoons orris root powder
2 tablespoons dried lemon peel
2 tablespoons dried sweet basil
4 tablespoons dried peppermint leaves
2 tablespoons dried rosemary
6 drops lavender oil
1 teaspoon gum benzoin

Combine all dried ingredients and, while gently tossing the mixture with one hand, add the oil, carefully, one drop at a time. Finally, gradually add the benzoin. Place in a covered jar and store in a warm, dark and dry place for 6 weeks, shaking the jar daily. Various colourful dried flowers may be added for extra richness of hue.

Sir Hugh's Delight

The following recipe was devised by Sir Hugh Platt of the Court of Elizabeth I and was published in his *Delights for Ladies*. The mixture was considered to have magical properties!

Lay scented flowers, roses and the like, and leaves in a box on a bed of dry sand and add more sand between each layer. (The flowers are left whole.) Place the box in the sun, avoiding both cooling and moisture. (The minimum time the box was left undisturbed was 21 days or "three times seven days". If, however, the roses were very fleshy, the time of drying was increased to "nine times nine".)

Fixatives were not then used, but if wished add a tablespoon of powdered orris, which incidentally has the aroma of violets, to a litre of whole dried roses.

Potpourri has been credited with much virtue. Centuries ago a particular mixture was considered an aphrodisiac and a bowl would be placed on a table outside the door of the bridal chamber. Anyone entering was expected to stir the bowl with the fourth finger of the left hand to release the stimulating fragrance. The herbs used were lemon verbena, marjoram, mint, thyme and violet, all sacred to Venus, and basil and broom, sacred to Mars. The same types of herbs were frequently strewn on the floor of the chamber so an amorous atmosphere would be created!

Sachets, Herbal Pillows and Sweet Bags

These all make very acceptable gifts. The sachets may be in almost any shape but always use fine cotton material to allow the fragrance to escape more readily. Sweet bags for the bath should be made of open weave cotton, fine netting being ideal, in order that the perfume is quickly released into the bath water. Herbal pillows are usually square or oblong.

Many men are grateful for such thoughtful items as herbal moth bags and "dry scented" sachets. The lavender potpourri would be appreciated by gentlemen to freshen their rooms, as the perfume is more astringent than that of most other potpourris.

Herbal Moth Bags

¼ cup dried mint
¼ cup dried wormwood
¼ cup dried tansy
¼ cup dried thyme
1 tablespoon crushed cinnamon

Simply combine all ingredients and place in bags to put among clothing in drawers. Sachets with a loop added can be hung among coats, dresses, and so on.

Dry Scented Sachet

1 tablespoon dried lemon balm
2 tablespoons dried lavender
2 tablespoons dried thyme

Unlike potpourri, sachets and moth bags do not require fixatives. Mix all the listed ingredients and fill sachet.

Herb Pillows

These, ranging in size from small sachets to bags 20 cm × 15 cm, may be filled with a mixture of any of the following dried herb leaves or flowers: dill, camomile, lemon verbena, mint, sage, bergamot, lavender, lemon balm, rose or geranium leaves and rosemary.

After filling the pillows, make another cover which can be easily removed for laundering. The outer cover may be "prettied up" with lace and touches of embroidery, perhaps even the recipient's initials.

Sweet Bags

Sweet bags for the bath may simply be squares of material tied with a ribbon to form a ball. Since they are used only once, minimum effort should be expended on making the bag. Good "bath" herbs are eau-de-Cologne mint, yarrow, camomile, elder flowers and leaves, rose petals and, of course, lavender. A box, prettily covered in attractive paper, could house perhaps a dozen of these tiny bags, but make sure that each is labelled with its ingredients. Half the fun for the lucky receiver would be to choose which of nature's gifts of fragrance would be added to the bath each day.

Other Gifts

Many other gifts may be made incorporating herbs. Imagine, for example, tiny "Raggedy Annes" filled with fragrance for some lucky child, or even stuffed animals with dried lavender or rosemary among the filling.

Coathangers are also acceptable and popular gifts and dried moth-repelling herbs such as rosemary, lavender, wormwood or tansy could be incorporated into the padding before the outer casing is stitched into place.

Herbal oils and vinegars too, have their place on the gift list. Always label each bottle clearly, naming the herb used. Jars of herbal salad dressings would also be appreciated. On the label, make sure instructions to refrigerate are given. A bottle of any of the herbal cordials would delight friends!

Stretch your imagination and you will be amazed at the variety and range of gifts that you can make from your herb patch. It may even be worth enquiring in specialty shops if there is a market for your products. In Australia many people are marketing herbal articles from home — think about it. It could prove to be a money-making hobby!

THE LANGUAGE OF HERBS, FLOWERS AND FRUIT
9

Through the ages various meanings have been attributed to many herbs, flowers and fruit. In the past a shy or bashful suitor would present the lady of his choice with a bouquet or nosegay of selected blooms which, if she understood the significance of each bloom, would convey his sentiments in the most aromatic and romantic manner. The language of flowers reached its zenith during the Victorian Age, which freely indulged in sentimentality. Though this is primarily a book about herbs, I have included many flower and fruit meanings as well in the following list. In times past, herbs, flowers and fruit blossoms were closely interwoven in their uses in both garden and still room. The "still" room was the special domain of the mistress of the house, where she prepared her potions, lotions and remedies, and dried herbs for use during the barren winter months. The following meanings are taken from the nineteenth century *Artistic Language of Flowers*, by an unknown author.

Almond	Hope
Angelica	Inspiration; magic
Balm	Sympathy
Basil, ornamental	Hatred
Basil, sweet	Good wishes; fidelity
Bay leaf	"I change but in death"
Bay tree	Glory
Bay wreath	Reward of merit
Borage	Bluntness
Cabbage	Profit
Calendula	Uneasiness; grief; despair
Camomile	Energy in adversity
Carnation, deep red	"Alas! for my poor heart"
Chicory	Frugality
Clover, four leafed	Be mine
Coriander	Hidden worth
Currant	"Thy frown will kill me"
Dandelion	Rustic oracle
Daphne	Glory; immortality
Dog rose	Pleasure and pain
Elder	Zealousness
Fennel	Worthy of all praise; strength
Fig tree	Prolific
Geranium, lemon	Unexpected meeting
Geranium, nutmeg	Unexpected meeting
Geranium, rose scented	Preference
Gilly flower (dianthus)	Bonds of affection
Gooseberry	Anticipation
Guelder rose	Winter
Heartsease or pansy	Thoughts
Heliotrope	Devotion, or "I turn to thee"
Hemlock	"You will be my death"
Hibiscus	Delicate beauty
Holly	Foresight
Hollyhock	Ambition; fecundity
Honeysuckle	Generous and devoted affection
House leek	Vivacity; domestic industry
Hyssop	Cleanliness
Iris	Message
Ivy	Friendship; fidelity; marriage
Jasmine	Amiability
Jasmine, Carolina	Separation
Jonquil	"I desire a return of affection"
Juniper	Succour; protection
Lavender	Distrust

**Top: Popular herbal gifts — sachets, sleep pillows,
and herb vinegar.**
Bottom: Dried and bottled herbs make an attractive display.

Left: French lavender.

Right: A corner of a garden which has been planted with herbs
and shrubs valued for their fragrant foliage or flowers.

THE LANGUAGE OF HERBS, FLOWERS AND FRUIT

Lemon	Zest
Lemon blossoms	Fidelity in love
Lettuce	Cold-heartedness
Lily of the valley	Return of happiness
Lime trees	Conjugal love
Marigold	Grief; despair
Marjoram	Blushes
Mignonette	"Your qualities surpass your charms"
Mint	Virtue
Mistletoe	"I surmount difficulties"
Mustard seed	Indifference
Myrrh	Gladness
Nasturtium	Patriotism
Oleander	Beware
Olive	Peace
Orange blossom	"Your purity equals your loveliness"
Parsley	Festivity
Pea, green	Departure
Peach	"Your qualities, like your charms, are unequalled"
Peach blossom	"I am your captive"
Pear	Affection
Pennyroyal	Flee away
Peppermint	Warmth of feeling
Periwinkle, blue	Early friendship
Periwinkle, white	Pleasures of memory
Persimmon	"Bury me among nature's beauties"
Pineapple	"You are perfect"
Pink, carnation	Woman's love
Pink, red, double	Pure and ardent love
Pink, single	Pure love
Pink, variegated	Refusal
Pink, white	Ingeniousness; talent
Plum tree	Fidelity
Polyanthus	Pride of riches
Quince	Temptation

Raspberry	Remorse
Rhododendron	Danger; beware
Rhubarb	Advice
Rocket	Rivalry
Rose	Love
Rose, burgundy	Unconscious beauty
Rose, cabbage	Ambassador of love
Rose, Carolina	"Love is dangerous"
Rose, China	Beauty always new
Rose, damask	Brilliant complexion
Rose, deep red	Bashful shame
Rose, moss	Love, voluptuousness
Rose, musk	Capricious beauty
Rose, single	Simplicity
Rose, thornless	Early attachment
Rose, white	"I am worthy of you"
Rose, yellow	Decrease of love; jealousy
Rose, York and Lancaster	War
Rose, red and white together	Unity
Rosebud, red	Pure and lovely
Rosebud, white	Girlhood
Rosemary	Remembrance
Rue	Repentance
Sage	Domestic virtue
Saint John's wort (hypericum)	Animosity
Snapdragon	Presumption
Snowdrop	Hope
Sorrel	Affection
Southernwood	Bantering
Spearmint	Warmth of sentiment
Speedwell	Female fidelity
Starwort, American	Cheerfulness in old age
Stephanotis	"Will you accompany me to the East?"
Stock	Lasting beauty
Sunflower, dwarf	Adoration

HERBS FOR THE HOME AND GARDEN

Sunflower, tall	Haughtiness
Sweetbriar, American	Simplicity
Sweetbriar, European	"I wound to heal"
Sweet pea	Delicate pleasures
Sweet William	Gallantry
Syringa, Carolina	Disappointment
Tansy	"I declare war against you"
Thyme	Activity or courage
Tuberose	Dangerous pleasure
Valerian	An accommodating disposition
Verbena, pink	Family happiness
Violet, blue	Faithfulness
Violet, sweet	Modesty
Violet, yellow	Rural happiness
Virginia creeper	"I cling to you both in sunshine and shade"
Wallflower	Fidelity in adversity
Watercress	Stability; power
Water lily	Purity in heart
Water melon	Bulkiness
Wormwood	Absence
Yarrow or milfoil	War

Origins of Significance

Angelica was believed to have been an inspired gift from an angel to a monk during a fearful plague as an antidote, hence "inspiration". The herb has, since earliest times, been thought to be proof against witchcraft and so we associate "magic" with the plant. Gerard believed angelica was the only herb with this power against witches.

Sweet basil is, in Italy, believed to represent fidelity whilst in other countries the purple or ornamental basil is considered to be a symbol of evil. In Keat's poem "Isabella or the Pot of Basil" the beautiful Isabella placed the head of her murdered lover in a pot of basil and watered it with her tears.

Bay wreaths were associated of course with glory. Glory in victory in battle or drama and poetry competitions. Even today we remember our fallen heroes with bay wreaths on memorials. The meaning of *camomile* is a little more subtle. It certainly shows "energy in adversity" as this ground-hugging herb grows far better if it is trodden on regularly.

Coriander's message of "hidden worth" quite possibly came from the fact that the seed must be crushed to release the superb flavour and delightful fragrance. *Dandelion* is truly a "rustic oracle" — few of us as children could refrain from blowing the soft globes to tell the time, inaccurate though it may have been! Anyone who has ever grown a *fig tree* will know that it is indeed a prolific bearer.

Shakespeare gave emphasis for the meaning of *pansies* when he had Ophelia say, ". . . and there is pansies, that's for thoughts". In fact, she was referring to a miniature form known then primarily as *heartsease*. The name "pansy" is a corruption of the French *pensée* meaning thought. The first true pansy that we know of today is believed to have been developed in a garden close to London about 150 years ago.

Hemlock's meaning, "you will be my death", is both blunt and to the point. It is extremely deadly. *Hyssop*, on the other hand, is regarded as the herb of cleanliness as we are told in the Bible in the Book of Leviticus, chapter XIV, that the priests used it as a purifying plant to cleanse lepers. Obviously *lemon* was allied to "zest" because of the flavour of its skin. When very finely peeled without any white pith, the yellow skin is frequently referred to as "zest".

The *lettuce*, of course, does have a cold heart, whether cut freshly from the garden or purchased from the supermarket. The *English Marigold's* meaning of grief and despair may have come from the impassioned cry of Charles I when imprisoned in Carisbrooke Castle:

"The marigold observes the Sun
More than my subjects me have done . . ."

"Blushes", the meaning of *marjoram*, could refer to the legend about Marjoram, a youth in the service of the king of Cyprus. One day he accidentally dropped a vial of costly perfumes. In a state of mortification and fear he lost consciousness and the gods changed him into the herb we enjoy using so much today.

Mint, meaning virtue, takes its name from Menthé, the beloved of Pluto. To keep Menthé from Pluto's advances, Pluto's wife, Proserpine, metamorphosed her and the herb bore the name of mint thereafter. *Myrrh*, with its message of gladness, was one of the rare spices taken by the Three Wise Men to present to the Christ Child.

Oleander is a shrub of which one must truly "beware". In the days of horse-drawn delivery vehicles it was used for street planting, as wise horses knew better than to chew on it. Every part is deadly poisonous. I recall my father-in-law telling of a roadside workman who boiled up his "billy" and made a pot of tea. Sugaring the pot, he stirred it with an oleander twig. Less than twenty-four hours later he was dead from the effects of the poison in the sap of the twig.

The *olive* has been a symbol of peace since Noah sent forth the dove which returned with the olive branch.

Parsley, representing festivity, is a reminder of how Greek and Roman revellers in ancient times would crown themselves with chaplets of parsley to ward off the effects of intoxication.

Pennyroyal means flee away — very appropriate when one realises that this tiny-leafed herb has the power to repel fleas. *Peppermint* has a "warmth of feeling" in its flavour and is the herb from which the oil of peppermint highly regarded by chemists and confectioners is extracted.

Roses are reminiscent of the Wars of the Roses, in which the houses of York (white rose) and Lancaster (red rose) fought with one another over which family would supply English monarchs. A mingling of the two roses resulted in a white and red rose, which represented the end of the feuding and became the emblem of the great House of Tudor.

Rosemary, signifying remembrance, brings to mind old Greek frescoes of students studying and wearing headbands into which are tucked sprigs of rosemary. This plant has long been associated with memory stimulation.

In Elizabethan times *rue* was associated with repentance as its bitter leaves reminded folk of those times of the bitterness of repentance. Most of us have heard the expression, "You'll rue the day", when some act which may require repentance has been committed. Country people of the sixteenth century believed that grace and forgiveness followed repentance and as a consequence we often hear of this herb of repentance being referred to as the "herb of grace o' Sundays".

Stephanotis is interesting with its meaning, "Will you accompany me to the East?". Considering that the most popular period for nosegays of flowers containing messages within their own beautiful forms came in Victorian England, I wonder if stephanotis received its meaning then. Many members of the army and civil service did cross the seas to the East and a posy of stephanotis may have been an acceptable way of asking that question of a young lady without fear of a verbal rebuff.

Thyme was believed by the ancient Greeks to give courage, and the name is a derivation of the Greek *thumos*, meaning courage.

The meaning of *wormwood*, "absence", could refer to its insect repelling properties.

Yarrow or *milfoil* represents war. This useful medicinal herb was considered an essential part of a British army surgeon's kit till the nineteenth century — it is invaluable in staunching bleeding.

Consider how interesting it would be to make a "meaningful" garden, choosing with care the appropriate herb, flower or fruit to convey personal sentiments to family and friends.

BIBLIOGRAPHY

Adamson, William. *Australian Gardener.* Mason & Firth, Melbourne, 1863.

Boland, Bridget. *Gardener's Magic and Other Old Wives' Lore.* The Bodley Head Ltd., London, 1977.

Bryan, J. E. and Coralie Castle. *The Edible Ornamental Garden.* Pitman Press, London, 1976.

Clarkson, R. E. *Herbs, Their Culture and Uses.* Macmillan, New York, 1971.

Culpeper, Nicholas. *Culpeper's Complete Herbal.* E. Ballard & Company, London, 1775.

Evelyn, John. *Acetaria: A Discourse on Sallets.*

Fox, Helen Morgenthau. *Gardening with Herbs.* Macmillan, New York, 1943.

Gerard, John. *The Herball.*

Hanle, Zack. *Cooking with Flowers.* Price/Stern/Sloan, Los Angeles, 1972.

Hatfield, Audrey Wynne. *Pleasures of Herbs.* Museum Press Ltd., London, 1964.

Hemphill, Rosemary. *Herbs for All Seasons.* Angus & Robertson, Sydney, 1972.

_____. *Herbs and Spices.* Penguin Books, London, 1966.

Hill, Sir John. *The Family Herbal.*
_____. *Virtues of British Herbs.*

Hyll, Thomas. *The Gardener's Labyrinth.*

Johnson, C. Pierpoint. *The Useful Plants of Great Britain.* William Kent & Co., London, 1862.

Kerr, Jessica. *Shakespeare's Flowers.* Kestral Books, Harmondsworth, Middlesex, 1969.

Lampard, M. (compiler). *From a Country Garden.* Marshall Cavendish Books Ltd., London, 1980.

Loewenfeld, Claire. *Herb Gardening.* Faber & Faber, London, 1964.

MacDonald, Christina. *Garden Herbs for Australia and New Zealand.* A. H. & A. W. Reed, Wellington, Sydney, London, 1969.

Parkinson, John. *Theatrum Botanicum.*

Philbrick, Helen and R. B. Gregg. *Companion Plants.* Stuart & Watkins, London, 1967.

Reid, Shirley. *Herbs for Australian Gardens and Kitchens.* Rigby Ltd., Adelaide, 1978.

Rohde, E. S. *A Garden of Herbs.* Rev. Edn, Dover, New York, 1969.

Sanders, T. W. *Encyclopaedia of Gardening.* Maclehone, London, 1895.

Senecki, K. H. *The Complete Book of Herbs.* Macdonald, London, 1974.

Webster, H. N. *Herbs: How to Grow Them and How to Use Them.* Charles T. Branford, Boston, 1939.

INDEX